HQ ARMY MATERIEL COMMAND REGULATION
HQ NAVAL SUPPLY SYSTEMS COMMAND INSTRUCTION
HQ AIR FORCE LOGISTICS COMMAND REGULATION
HEADQUARTERS US MARINE CORPS ORDER

AMC-R 700–99
NAVSUPINST 4790.7
AFLCR 400–21
MCO P4410.22C

LOGISTICS

WHOLESALE INVENTORY MANAGEMENT AND LOGISTICS SUPPORT OF MULTISERVICE USED NONCONSUMABLE ITEMS

27 April 1990

DEPARTMENTS OF THE ARMY, THE NAVY, AND THE AIR FORCE

DEPARTMENT OF THE ARMY, THE NAVY, AND THE AIR FORCE

Headquarters Army Materiel Command   AMC-R 700-99
5001 Eisenhower Ave
Alexandria Va 22333-0001

Headquarters Naval Supply Systems Command   NAVSUPINST 4790.7
Crystal City, Washington DC 20376-5000

Headquarters Air Force Logistics Command   AFLCR 400-21
Wright-Patterson Air Force Base OH 45433-5001

Headquarters US Marine Corps   MCO P4410.22C
Washington DC 20380-0001   27 April 1990

Logistics

**WHOLESALE INVENTORY MANAGEMENT AND LOGISTICS SUPPORT OF
MULTISERVICE USED NONCONSUMABLE ITEMS**

Supplements to this regulation are prohibited. Send suggestions or changes required
to this regulation to the command office of primary responsibility (OPR).

Purpose. This publication provides the procedures which the logistics elements of the
military services have established to accomplish the intent of FY 74 Department of
Defense (DOD) Management Objective 8, Action 6: Eliminate Duplicate Wholesale
Inventory Management as it applies to nonconsumable items. The procedures provide for
the actions to be accomplished in two separate but related phases. Phase I, completed
December 1976, resulted in a single manager assignment of responsibility for
cataloging, procurement, disposal, and, where appropriate, depot level maintenance
(maintenance to be accomplished by Depot Maintenance Interservice Support Agreement).
Phase II provides for a single wholesale manager for depot reparable components and a
single wholesale stock for all users. Upon completion of all actions contained in
this publication, each affected National Stock Numbered nonconsumable item will have a
single DOD wholesale manager. Ammunition, cryptological, and nuclear items, while
excluded from the purview of this publication, will be addressed by the cognizant
agencies/activities. While government agencies outside of the DOD, such as the
Federal Aviation Administration and Coast Guard are not bound by this regulation, they
are encouraged to participate in the program as negotiated with the military services
to obtain support and eliminate duplication in the logistics management of jointly
used nonconsumables.

<table>
<tr><td></td><td>Paragraph</td><td>Page</td></tr>
<tr><td>Chapter 1 - Introduction</td><td></td><td></td></tr>
<tr><td>Background. . . . .</td><td>1-1</td><td>4</td></tr>
<tr><td>Purpose . . . .</td><td>1-2</td><td>5</td></tr>
<tr><td>Objectives. . . . .</td><td>1-3</td><td>5</td></tr>
<tr><td>Scope . . . .</td><td>1-4</td><td>5</td></tr>
<tr><td>Responsibilities. . . . .</td><td>1-5</td><td>6</td></tr>
<tr><td>Nonconsumable Item Materiel Support Codes (NIMSC) . . . . . .</td><td>1-6</td><td>8</td></tr>
</table>

Supersedes AFLCR 400-21/DARCOM-R 700-99/NAVMATINST 4790.23B/MCO P4410.22B, 25 Feb
1982.
(See signature page for summary of changes.) No. of Printed Pages: 62 OPR: AMC/
AMCSM-MSM
          NAVSUP/0632
          AFLC/MMI - Lead Command
          USMC/LPP-2
          Distribution: (See Page 37)

Chapter 1

INTRODUCTION

1-1. Background:
a. The Joint Logistics Commanders (JLCs) directed their Joint Policy Coordinating Group for Defense Integrated Materiel Management (JPCG/DIMM) to eliminate unnecessary duplication in the management and logistics support of multiservice nonconsumable used items. The JPCG/DIMM, in February 1974, chartered a Nonconsumable Item Subgroup (NIS) to do this.

b. The Deputy Secretary of Defense (DEPSECDEF), by issuing a Memorandum for the Secretaries of the Military Departments, dated 30 March 1974, DOD Management Objective 8, Action 6: Eliminate Duplicate Wholesale Inventory Management, directed the military services to continue with the JLC ongoing effort, but to observe certain specific guidance which directed that:

(1) All nonconsumable items used by two or more services will be identified and reviewed to determine which service should be the materiel manager of the item or to identify and justify any other valid exceptional management arrangements.

(2) Assignment of materiel management responsibility will be weighted heavily in favor of the service having the largest technical and depot maintenance capability supporting the item and will consider the capabilities of the service initially developing the items.

(3) Assignment of materiel management responsibility to a service will include the functions of computation of replacement and overhaul requirements, budgeting and funding, procurement, receipt, storage and issue, depot level maintenance, cataloging, and disposal.

(4) Piecemeal assignments of materiel management functions for the same items won't be given to any service. c. The JLC, in response to the 30 March 1974 DEPSECDEF memorandum, developed an alternate two-phased program and recommended its approval for implementation. The functions of computing retail requirements and budgeting and funding for retail levels are retained by the individual services under the alternate two-phased program.

d. The Office of the Assistant Secretary of Defense (OASD), by memorandum dated 27 November 1974, directed that the implementation of Phase I, under the auspices of the JLC, should proceed. By memorandum dated 5 February 1975, the OASD approved the alternate program recommended by the JLC and directed action be taken to proceed with the planning for implementation of Phase II. OASD memorandum dated 10 May 1976 approved the Phase II plan and directed that all necessary resources should be made available to ensure the development and implementation of Phase II.

e. Implementation of Phase I resulted in a lead service, referred to as the Primary Inventory Control Activity (PICA), assignment to each National Stock Numbered (NSN) nonconsumable item in the total item record (TIR) file of the Federal records at the Defense Logistics Service Center (DLSC) with the exception of those items identified in paragraph 1-4b below. Functional responsibilities (for multiservice used nonconsumables) assigned to the PICA under Phase I (Type I Support) were limited to single submitter of cataloging data, procurement and disposal authority, and depot level maintenance authority. For single service used nonconsumables, the PICA assignment was made to the single user and item management responsibilities cover the total logistics spectrum. Consistently managed support equipment end items won't be reviewed for migration to Phase II. Inconsistently managed end items will be reviewed for Phase II according to chapter 3 of this regulation.

f. Implementation of Phase II (Type II Support) adds additional responsibilities to the PICA which will result in a single wholesale manager for each affected depot reparable component and a single wholesale stock for all users. The procedures and degree of these responsibilities are included in chapter 3. It should be stressed that while the wholesale manager is identified as a PICA, the responsibilities assigned include functions that may not reside in the item management organization. When such is the case, the PICA will make sure the work is done by the cognizant organization.

g. As part of objective 8, the JPCG/DIMM chartered the Interchangeable and Substitutable Item Subgroup (ISIS) to select a single service as manager for each I&S family grouping. The ISIS was disestablished in 1984, and the DOD Interchangeability and Substitutability (I&S) committee took over its functions.

Procedures to implement interservice I&S objectives, for both consumable and nonconsumable items are contained in AFLCR 400-31/AMC-R 700-30/NAVSUPINST 4400.25/MCO 4410.24/DLA-R 4140.66.

h. In July 1985, the JLC directed that the JPCH/DIMM continue to perform their joint tasks on a normal staff-to-staff basis. They will meet as required at the request of any of the service members or the JLC. The chairmanship will rotate among the services yearly. The Nonconsumable Item Subgroup (NIS) has been replaced by a staff-to-staff working level group called the Nonconsumable Item Program Committee (NIPC). This committee meets quarterly and will rotate the chairmanship among the services yearly. Their functions are to implement and monitor the Nonconsumable Item Program and administer this publication.

i. In support of this program, the Maintenance Interservice Support Management Offices (MISMOs) established within the military services by OPNAVINST 4790.13/AMC-R 750-10/ AFLCR 800-30/AFSCR 800-30/MCO P4790.10A will review weapon systems, equipment end items, systems, subsystems, components, or commodity groups meeting at least one of the following criteria prior to assignment of depot maintenance responsibility and/or expenditure of funds for depot hardware acquisition or depot facilitization. For purposes of review criteria, interim contractor logistics support for a finite period is not an assignment of depot maintenance responsibility.

(1) New system or equipment acquisitions or modification programs requiring depot maintenance (DM) support.

(2) System or equipment depot repair programs being planned for transition from contract support to organic support or organic support to contract support.

(3) Existing system or equipment for which an expansion in depot level capability requires an additional depot capital investment of $100,000 or more.

(4) Jointly used or managed system or equipment planned for introduction into the DOD for which depot maintenance support is required.

(5) Proposed or planned realignment of DM workloads which affect published depot maintenance interservice (DMI) decisions or DMI studies currently under way. This review criterion is applicable to intraservice changes or additions for existing DMI decisions if the $100,000 or more capital investment requirement is met.

(6) Items repaired on contract will be considered by the contracting Service for DMI support upon expiration/termination of contract and prior to contract renewal. Time must be allowed prior to contract expiration/termination to permit the DMI assessment to be completed and documented.

1-2. Purpose. This publication provides uniform guidance and procedures for applying PICA materiel management assignment criteria, as delineated here, so that one service will provide certain logistics support functions to all military users of nonconsumable items.

1-3. Objectives:

a. Eliminate duplication in the wholesale materiel management of nonconsumable items.

b. Provide effective and efficient interservice wholesale supply and depot level maintenance support of nonconsumable items.

c. Use existing DOD standard systems and procedures to the maximum extent practicable.

d. Preclude future item management duplication of multiservice used nonconsumable items.

e. Review inconsistently managed items and establish materiel and financial management consistency whenever practical.

f. Ensure equal treatment to all customers without regard to service/agency lines.

g. Maintain continuity of supply support during transition of applicable management functions.

h. Incorporate, insofar as practicable Automated Data Processing (ADP) techniques in support of this program to minimize manual processing and/or handling.

i. Expedite the return of unserviceable assets to the wholesale level.

1-4. Scope:

a. This publication provides the necessary guidance to implement a program whereby each national stock numbered nonconsumable item will be assigned to a single military service for PICA management except for those exclusions covered in the following paragraph.

b. Items under the management cognizance of the Defense Nuclear Agency (DNA), National Security Agency (NSA), and the services' Joint Conventional Ammunition Production Coordinating Group (JCAP-CG) are excluded from the purview of this publication.

These agencies/activities are encouraged to work within the parameters of this regulation to the extent possible and will issue internal procedures to eliminate duplication associated with multiservice used nonconsumables. Specific items to be excluded are:

    (1) Conventional ammunition items in Federal Supply Group (FSG) 13 under cognizance of JCAP-CG.

    (2) By direction of the Assistant Secretary of Defense (ASD) all nuclear ordnance items in Federal Supply Group (FSG) 11 and items regardless of Federal Supply Classification (FSC) with Commercial and Government Entity (CAGE) 57991, 67991, 77991, and 87991 will be under the cognizance of the Defense Nuclear Agency (DNA).

    (3) Cryptological items identified in FSC 5810 and 5811, items with Commercial and Government Entity (CAGE) 02227, 11874, 15942, 28865, or 98230, and items regardless of class under cognizance of the NSA. NSA/CSS Circular 62-2, Change 1, dated 27 December 1979, Integrated Materiel Management of Cryptological Nonconsumable Items applies. (Items in these categories not under the cognizance of NSA will be processed according to this publication.)

    (4) Multiservice used nonconsumables which have been identified as having I&S relationships are being addressed by the DOD I&S Committee. As items having I&S relationships are assigned level of authority (LOA) 22/8D status, they will become subject to the provisions of this regulation.

  c. Ships, aircraft and other major end items for which management and control are exercised through the application of unique identification systems are exempt from this program.

  d. Construction and materiel handling equipment will be jointly procured as directed by AFLCR 73-3/AMC-R 715-6/NAVSUPINST 11260.1A/MCO 4200.25A/DLAR 4145.34.

  e. The implementation of this program recognizes the following item management concepts and organizational entities:

    (1) Responsibility for multiservice used consistently managed support equipment will not normally be expanded beyond Phase I Management.

    (2) Materiel management functions, not assigned to the PICA, will be the responsibility of the secondary inventory control activity (SICA) service.

    (3) A PICA will be assigned for each inconsistently managed item.

(Inconsistent items are those which are managed by the military services in some combination of end items, depot reparable components, consumables and special management items.) The service that manages this type item as a depot reparable component will normally be assigned as the PICA.

    (4) Because of the entirely different concepts the Navy and Air Force use in managing air launched missiles, all Navy PICA items identified with Navy cognizant symbol 8E will remain under Phase I and not be processed into Phase II.

    (5) Depot Maintenance Interservice Support Agreements (DMISAs) will be negotiated between the involved services for all items where depot level maintenance is required by the SICA and the PICA does not perform wholesale stock, store, and issue with credit/exchange for the affected SICA. Any exceptions to the maintenance assignment will be documented and submitted to the SICA service MISMO for Joint MISMO resolution.

    (6) Certificates of Usability are required on items wherein the PICA has provided a technical package to the SICA for review and the SICA has agreed to wholesale stock, store and issue functions being performed by the PICA.

    (7) Assignment of depot level maintenance will be through the DMI Program as defined in OPNAVINST 4790.14, AMC-R 750-10, AFLCR/AFSCR 800-30, MCO P4790.10A, Logistics Depot Maintenance's Interservice.

    (8) The approved depot source of repair (DSOR) will be identified by the Service's Maintenance Interservice Support Management Office (MISMO) to the PICA for inclusion in the Defense Integrated Data System Total Item Record (DIDS TIR).

  f. The procedures contained in this publication provide for implementation and subsequent operation.

1-5. Responsibilities:

  a. Each military service is responsible for:

    (1) Providing representation to the JPCG-DIMM and NIPC.

    (2) Providing a service focal point responsible for receiving and monitoring data required for the implementation of this program.

    (3) Revising its internal procedures, as applicable, to accommodate the procedures contained herein and accomplish the objectives.

(4) Implementing the required actions.

(5) Assuming or relinquishing applicable materiel management responsibilities on an established effective date.

(6) Developing the necessary internal procedures to implement the materiel returns program whereby transactions can be processed and controlled across service lines to account for assets returned under a credit/exchange arrangement and excess assets.

b. JPCG/DIMM is responsible for:

(1) Establishing interservice policies and procedures for eliminating unnecessary duplication in the wholesale materiel management of nonconsumable items.

(2) Providing guidance and reviewing actions taken by the NIPC.

(3) Resolving issues referred by the NIPC.

(4) Reviewing and resolving interservice materiel management problems when tasked by the JLC.

c. NIPC is responsible for:

(1) Developing the procedures and an implementation program for the assignment of a PICA for all affected nonconsumable items.

(2) Developing joint operational publications for use by the military services in the management of items designated under this program.

(3) Providing program monitorship to make sure all actions required to implement this program are completed.

(4) Ensuring that the DLSC TIR is updated to reflect the PICA/SICA relationship with the appropriate Major Organizational Entity (MOE) or LOA rules and Nonconsumable Item Materiel Support Codes (NIMSCs).

(5) Resolving issues between the services and referring those which cannot be resolved at the NIPC level to the JPCG/DIMM or JLC.

d. Military Service Inventory Control Points (ICP) are responsible for:

(1) Establishing a central monitor to receive data and ensure timely local processing.

(2) Establishing detailed procedures for program implementation and participating in periodic technical reviews, as required.

(3) Establishing schedules for review of items assigned to determine if items should migrate to Type II management.

(4) Establishing the NIMSC desired in coordination with its own service technical activity/function for each item when acting as SICA.

(5) Initiating action to update applicable Catalog Management Data (CMD) record in the DLSC TIR in accordance with DOD 4100.39M.

(6) Developing necessary instructions and establishing training programs as required.

(7) Assuming the responsibilities for the logistics functions on effective transfer date and recording of PICA assignment in the DLSC TIR.

(8) Referring policy or problem issues which develop between service ICPs to their respective NIPC member for resolution.

e. MISMOs are responsible for:

(1) Reviewing NSNs in the service inventories common to two or more services where depot level maintenance is involved in at least one service.

(2) Selecting the military service(s) to accomplish the total maintenance requirement.

(3) Reviewing maintenance assignments and PICA/SICA relationships as required by individual ICPs.

(4) Depot maintenance assignments for nonconsumable items, including end items (principal and secondary) and components, are joint service maintenance decisions and are not to be changed by either the PICA or SICA without another joint service maintenance review by the MISMO. The depot maintenance assignment may be to a service other than the PICA service.

(5) Providing DSOR assignment information to the PICA ICP for inclusion in the DIDS TIR.

f. PICA will be responsible for:

(1) Single submitter for cataloging segment B or DLSC TIR, except for exclusions identified in paragraph 1-4b.

(2) Authorizing procurement and/or processing the procurement instrument, when applicable, for all items assigned.

(3) Determining DOD excess position on items assigned and initiating appropriate disposal action.

(4) Determining wholesale stock levels required to support military service users for assigned items.

(5) Establishing, in conjunction with the SICA, the degree of nonconsumable item materiel support to be provided as indicated by the NIMSC.

(6) Providing support to the SICA(s) in accordance with the negotiated degree of nonconsumable item materiel support.

(7) Negotiating DMISAs when required.

(8) Identifying program/item data required from SICA in correlation with the degree of materiel support to be provided.

(9) Processing all MISMO interservice maintenance assignments. Maintenance responsibility resides within the PICA but actual maintenance may be performed by another service or by commercial contract as designated by the NIMSC.

(10) Recording the applicable PICA NIMSC in the DLSC TIR to reflect the depot maintenance support arrangement.

(11) Notifying SICA of the maintenance activity responsible for depot repair.

(12) Establishing PICA service requirements.

(13) Budgeting and funding for service requirements in accordance with materiel support codes assigned.

(14) Recording PICA and SICA DSOR codes, as approved by the Service MISMOs, in the DIDS TIR to reflect the authorized depot source of repair.

g. SICA will be responsible for:

(1) Submitting request for acquisition of items to the assigned PICA.

(2) Notifying the PICA of service excesses and taking proper disposition action.

(3) Negotiating with the PICA the level of support required by the SICA and the appropriate NIMSC to reflect the level of support using Phase II to the maximum extent practical.

(4) Providing the PICA, on a cyclic basis, projected requisitioning requirements and projected unserviceable returns.

(5) Submitting to the PICA the applicable NIMSC to update the DLSC TIR.

(6) Submitting to the PICA proposed cataloging changes to data under the PICA's cognizance according to DOD 4100.39M.

(7) Negotiating DMISA with the PICA when depot repair is desired for items assigned NIMSC codes other than 1,2,5 or 6.

(8) Providing program item data to the PICA when required by the PICA to meet the materiel support commitments.

(9) Establishing SICA service requirements.

(10) Budgeting and funding for service requirements in accordance with materiel support codes assigned.

(11) Providing DSOR codes approved by the SICA service MISMO to the PICA ICP for recording in the DIDSTIR.

1-6. Nonconsumable Item Materiel Support Codes (NIMSC). NIMSCs will be entered in the TIR files at DLSC by the PICA. Numeric codes apply only to the SICA record and identify the materiel support relationship when the SICA level of authority (LOA) is 8D. The numeric code reflects the wholesale logistics functions which are to be performed by the PICA in support of the SICA. Alpha codes are applicable only to PICA records and identify the PICA source(s) for doing depot maintenance or other depot maintenance arrangement. NOTE: For NIMSCs 1,2,3,4,5,8, and 9 the SICA catalog management data (CMD) will reflect source of supply or source of supply modifiers compatible with the SICA managing activity. The PICA will not be entered in the Defense Automated Addressing System (DAAS) Integrated Materiel Manager (IMM) field. For NIMSC 6, SICA CMD will reflect the source of supply or source of supply modifier compatible with the PICA managing activity and may reflect the Acquisition Advice Code (AAC) of the PICA. The PICA will not be entered in the DAASIMM field.

Code Definition:

1 Exception Item (End Item of Equipment). This code   identifies SICA managed end items of equipment assigned to   another service PICA that is responsible for the wholesale   logistics support functions of single submitter of cataloging   data, acquisition and disposal authority. Supply support   requirements will be submitted by the SICA to the PICA on   Military Interdepartmental Purchase Requests (MIPRs) unless   otherwise directed by the PICA. The SICA is responsible for   the wholesale stock, store, and issue functions, in support of   SICA activities and has retained depot repair capability where applicable. Retention of depot maintenance capability   for end items of equipment requires documented justification by the SICA to the PICA via JLC Form 19. If PICA and SICA   cannot reach an agreement the documentation will be forwarded   to the joint MISMOs for a decision.

2 Exception Item (Depot Reparable Component or SICA Managed   Consumable). This code identifies SICA managed depot reparable components or SICA managed consumables wherein the   SICA cannot use repaired items, assigned to another service which has responsibility for the logistics functions of

single submitter of cataloging data, acquisition and disposal authority. Supply support requirements will be submitted by the SICA to the PICA on MIPRs unless otherwise directed by PICA. The SICA service has retained the wholesale stock, store, and issue functions in support of SICA activities and has retained depot repair capability, where applicable. Retention of depot maintenance capability for the depot reparable components requires documented justification by the SICA to the PICA via JLC Form 19. If the PICA and SICA cannot reach an agreement, the documentation will be forwarded to the joint MISMOs for a decision.

3 End Item Primary Inventory Control Activity. This code identifies SICA managed end items or equipment assigned to another service PICA that is responsible for the wholesale logistics support functions of single submitter of cataloging data, acquisition and disposal authority and depot maintenance, if required, to be provided by DMISA. Supply support requirements will be submitted by the SICA to the PICA on MIPRs unless otherwise directed by PICA. The SICA is responsible for the wholesale stock, store, and issue functions for SICA activities.

4 Depot Reparable Component. (Type I Temporary). This code identifies SICA managed depot reparable components assigned to another service PICA that is responsible for the logistics functions of single submitter of cataloging data, acquisition and disposal authority and depot maintenance to be provided by DMISA. Supply support requirements will be submitted by the SICA to the PICA on MIPRs unless otherwise directed by the PICA. The SICA is responsible for the wholesale stock, store and issue functions for SICA activities. This code is temporarily assigned to items which have not completed Phase II item review processing.

5 Depot Reparable Component (Type II). This code identifies SICA managed depot reparable components assigned to another service which is responsible for the logistics functions of single submitter cataloger, acquisition and disposal authority, depot maintenance, and performs the wholesale stock, store, and issue functions and establishes, budgets, and funds the wholesale stock level requirement. Supply requirements will be submitted to the PICA on requisitions which are funded by a designated point within the SICA. Unserviceable SICA assets will normally be returned to the PICA for credit. The SICA will provide item/program data required by the PICA to meet the materiel support commitments. Normally, Military Interdepartmental Purchase Requests (MIPR) will not be requested by the PICA to support SICA NIMSC 5 requirements.

6 Requisitioning Activity Funded Items. This code identifies items wherein SICA activities have been authorized by their parent service to submit requisitions directly to the PICA. These items are usually managed as consumable (expense) items by the SICA service.

7 JCAP Cognizance. This item is under JCAP cognizance and supply support will be determined by the DOD Single Manager for Conventional Ammunition. Provisions of this regulation will not apply.

8 Depot Reparable Component (Type I). This code identifies SICA managed depot reparable components which have been reviewed for migration to Type II, but will be retained under Type I management. The PICA will have responsibility for the logistics functions of single submitter of cataloging data, acquisition and disposal authority, and depot maintenance to be provided by DMISA. Supply support requirements will be submitted by the SICA to the PICA via MIPRs unless otherwise directed by the PICA. The SICA is responsible for wholesale stock, store, and issue functions for SICA activities.

9 Exception Item (Depot Maintenance Review Not Completed). This code identifies items wherein assignment for depot repair has not been established. PICA responsibilities are limited to single submitter of cataloging data, acquisition and disposal authority. Upon completion of depot maintenance review, and assignment for depot repair is made, code 9 items will be reassigned to code 1,2,3,5,6, or 8.

O DLSC File Conversion Code. This code was assigned by DLSC to existing wholesale interservice supply support agreement (WISSA) type recording (LOA 8D) during initial file conversion program. This code is reassigned to code 1,2,3,5,6, or 8 upon completion of item review.

A An activity within the Army is providing depot maintenance support.

B Multiservice Organic Repair. The depot repair requirement of two or more services is being performed organically by more than one service.

E Excess overflow which is contracted by the PICA.

F An activity within the Air Force is providing depot maintenance support.

J JCAP Cognizance. This item is under JCAP cognizance and supply support will be determined by the DOD single manager for conventional ammunition. Provisions of this regulation won't apply.

M An activity within the Marine Corps is providing depot maintenance support.

P Total depot maintenance is being done by commercial contract.

S Organic overflow to another service possessing organic capability.

U Unassigned. MISMO review not completed. Current depot repair arrangements remain in effect.

V An activity within the Navy is providing depot maintenance support.

X All other conditions.

1-7. Existing Agreements. WISSAs between or among the military services currently in effect will be considered superseded upon implementation of this program and recording of applicable NIMSCs in the DLSC TIR.

1-8. Precedent. The policies and procedures described here reflect the current joint position on nonconsumable items. Where individual service regulations and this regulation are in conflict, the provisions of this regulation will apply.

1-9. Changes to Publication:
 a. Recommended changes may be submitted as need arises by affected service activities. All recommendations for additions, deletions, and corrections, including inquiries or correspondence regarding implementation of the procedures and functional processes stated herein or in the cited directive, will be processed through the chain of command to the following points of contact for joint service staffing:

 (1) US Army US Army Materiel Command ATTN: AMCSM-MSM 5001 Eisenhower Avenue Alexandria, VA. 22333-0001

 (2) US Navy NAVAL Supply Systems Command SUP 0632 Washington DC 20376-5000

 (3) US Air Force HQ Air Force Logistics Command/MMIII Wright-Patterson AFB OH 45433-5001

 (4) US Marine Corps Commandant of the Marine Corps HQ USMC/LPP-2 Washington DC 20380-0001

 b. Identity recommendations or comments to the specific page, paragraph, and line in the text. The proposed revised text should include sufficient rationale for the recommended change(s).

 1-10. Forms. Each form covered by this regulation may be reproduced locally.

SUPPLY AND DEPOT MAINTENANCE OPERATIONS   (NIMSC 1,2,3,4,8, OR 9)

2-1. General. Procedures contained in this chapter will be used by the designated PICA and by the SICA for NIMSCs 1,2,3,4, 8, or 9. Each service will determine requirements and budget and fund in support of its needs.

2-2. Engineering and Technical Data. Each military service will retain engineering and technical authority in support of its own equipment/systems. The service assigned to perform depot maintenance will provide a negotiated maintenance work specification as part of the DMISA. The SICA will make sure the acquisition and technical data are incorporated in the package provided to the PICA. If any proposed change would result in the establishment of a new item and if user concurrence cannot be obtained, separate items of supply will be established; that is, two separate identifying NSNs.

2-3. Provisioning. Provisioning of new systems/equipment or the adoption for the use of systems/equipment in DOD inventory is the responsibility of each service. Nonconsumable items being introduced into the DOD inventory will be assigned to the introducing service for PICA management. Where joint provisioning is being accomplished by two or more services, PICA management assignment of nonconsumable items will be in accordance with paragraph 5-2. Requirements for nonconsumable items, established during provisioning which are already assigned to a PICA, will be submitted to the PICA via Nonconsumable Item Materiel Support Request (NIMSR) for support.

2-4. Item Adoption. PICAs will not register SICAs prior to receiving a NIMSR from the SICA. A service that has a requirement for and desires to adopt an item previously assigned to a PICA will:

a. Request materiel support from the PICA via NIMSR (appendix D).

b. Negotiate the degree of support desired with the PICA.

c. Provide the necessary data to the PICA so that the PICA may update the total item record to reflect user interest and applicable MOE rules.

d. Negotiate a DMISA with the PICA for depot repair, if required.

e. Provide the PICA with any additional data required by the PICA to insure subsequent support.

2-5. Procurement:

a. **Responsibilities.** The PICA is responsible for the acquisition of all items of supply under their cognizance. The SICA will be responsible for forwarding MIPRs to the PICA for all quantities of the item required by the SICA service. Funded or unfunded requisitions may be used by the SICA with the concurrence of the PICA. Before submission of a MIPR or Military Standard Requisitioning and Issue Procedures (MILSTRIP) requisition, the SICA will contact the PICA to determine which funding document is required. Prior to initiating procurement actions on the SICA's requirements, the PICA will check their own available wholesale stocks, as well as query the other SICA users (see para 2-5b(1)(d), and attempt to fill the requirement out of available stocks, based upon the same priorities they would apply to their own service requisitions.

b. **Procedures.**

(1) The PICA will:

(a) Conduct or direct acquisition of assigned items using existing service acquisition procedures in accordance with the Federal Acquisition Regulation (FAR).

(b) Provide SICA(s) with estimated delivery dates.

(c) Administer the priorities and allocate authority in the purchase of the assigned items through established channels in accordance with DODI 4400.1, Department of Defense Priorities and Allocations.

(d) In accordance with DOD 4160.21-M, chapter IV, query all other military services maintaining wholesale stocks for asset availability before beginning procurement actions. Interrogation may be conducted by telephone, message or mail based on the urgency involved (see below). The number of items in each telephone inquiry should be kept to a minimum, and all telephone inquiries must be recorded by both Inventory Control Points (ICPs) involved to ensure accurate reporting of completed transactions. Interrogations will be prepared in accordance with appendix G, and will be identified by a J in the first position of the document serial number. The types of interrogations based on priority are:

1. Emergency Requirement Interrogation. Needed to fill demands for issue priorities 01-03. Asset availability information is required within 36 hours.

2. Urgent Requirement Interrogation. Needed to fill demands for issue priority 04-08. Asset availability information is required within 72 hours.

3. Routine Requirement Interrogation. Needed to fill demands for issue priorities 09-15 and current year buy and repair requirements. Asset availability information is required within 10 days.

(e) When notification of asset availability is received, the PICA will determine if those assets will meet their requirement. If so, the PICA should submit a MILSTRIP requisition with the Interrogation Document Number in CC 30-43 and 2J advice code in CC 65-66. If the assets cannot be utilized, the PICA will notify the SICA of the rejection by letter or message. Appropriate data records will be retained to verify that prior inquiries of other users were made before purchase. In compliance with the provisions of the Federal Acquisition Regulation (FAR), the Purchase Requests (PRs) or Military Interdepartmental Purchase Requests (MIPRs) generated will contain the following certification: "DOD policies for the utilization of releasable assets as set forth in DOD 4160.21-M have been complied with. Document Number_____ applies." This certification is not required on PRs/ MIPRs with a dollar value under $50.00 or for items used by a single service.

(f) Request and consolidate any available procurement source and pricing information from all other service users prior to initiating new procurements.

(2) The SICA will:

(a) Assure that PICA centrally procured items are not purchased by requiring activities under their control, except when authorized by the PICA. In case of emergency requirements, the purchase action will be limited to immediate use quantity. When emergency or PICA authorized purchases are made one copy of the contractual instrument plus any available source and pricing information should be forwarded promptly to the appropriate PICA.

(b) Reply to PICA interrogations for assets in accordance with time frames outlined in paragraph 2-5b(1)(d) and in the format contained in appendix G. In reply

to interrogations, the original interrogation document number will always be referenced and complete information concerning available materiel, including quantity, condition, and funding requirements, will be provided to the PICA ICP. Activities receiving interrogation requests will respond as follows:

1. Emergency Interrogation (priorities 01-03). Make all on-hand assets available to the same extent that you would to satisfy your own service requirements.

2. Urgent Interrogation (PRI 04-08). Make every effort to satisfy the urgent requirement, either reimbursable or nonreimbursable.

3. Routine Interrogation (PRI 08-15 and current year buy/repair requirements). Offer those on-hand assets above the Approved Force Acquisition Objective (AFAO) on a nonreimbursable basis.

2-6. Cataloging:

a. Responsibilities:

(1) The PICA will be the single submitter of cataloging data for each item assigned. SICA proposed changes to item data which are the responsibility of the PICA as the single submitter of cataloging data will be submitted to the PICA for processing. The PICA will:

(a) Review and determine the proper actions.

(b) Collaborate with all users as required by DOD 4100.39M, DIDS Procedures Manual.

(c) Resolve all conflicts from collaboration prior to submittal to DLSC.

(d) Submit the proposed action to DLSC.

(2) The service MISMOs are the only approval authority for assignment, change, or deletions of DSOR codes in the DIDS TIR.

(3) DLSC will process those item changes applicable to the user registration segment of the DLSC TIR only when received from the PICA.

(4) The PICA will be uniquely identified by a PICA MOE rule with an LOA 22. The SICAs will be uniquely identified by a SICA MOE rule with an LOA 8D.

(5) Subsequent to PICA registration in DLSC, additional requests for PICA registration action on an existing PICA managed nonconsumable item will be rejected and returned to the submitting activity for resubmittal to the recorded PICA.

(6) All cataloging actions will be in accordance with DOD 4100.39-M.

b. Procedures.

(1) For new items entering the system, the service introducing the item will request and be recorded in the DLSC TIR with the appropriate PICA MOE rule, LOA, NIMSC, and DSOR.

(2) When another service desires to adopt an established item, a NIMSR will be submitted to the PICA indicating the appropriate MOE rule, NIMSC, and other information.

c. PICAs and SICAs will input their individual service Catalog Management Data (CMD) directly to DLSC in accordance with DOD 4100.39-M, except proposed Management Level Changes (MLC) which would impact on SICA service.

d. NIMSCs and the DSORs will be entered in Segment B of the DLSC TIR.

e. To establish or change MOE rules or NIMSC, the SICA must submit the requirement to the PICA for input to DLSC.

f. When the LOA is changing from consumable (06) to nonconsumable (22) or vice versa, cataloging changes impacting another service will not be made without collaboration and concurrence with all services involved using JLC Form 19.

g. PICAs desiring to transfer management responsibility to another service will send a JLC Form 19 to the predominant user. After the predominant user's acceptance, a copy of the completed JLC Form 19 will be forwarded to the other users for information/action.

h. SICAs desiring to gain management responsibility will send a JLC Form 19 to the current PICA. After the current PICA's acceptance, the completed JLC Form 19 will be forwarded to the other users for information/action. The gaining PICA will inform all SICAs upon adoption.

2-7. Depot Maintenance:

a. Selection of the service/activity to perform the depot maintenance of a nonconsumable item is the responsibility of the Joint MISMOS. In support of this program, the MISMOs or their designated representative will review all multiservice used nonconsumable items and selected new single service used systems, end items and components which are subject to depot repair. Upon determination of the depot sources of repair, each service will process the DSOR Code information to its ICP as outlined herein and in OPNAVINST 4790.14, AMC-4 750-10, AFLCR/AFSCR 800-30, MCO P4790.10A.

b. The PICA is responsible for the maintenance of the nonconsumable items to which assigned. In those instances where another service performs depot level maintenance, that service will be responsible to the PICA for accomplishment as required. This arrangement will be documented an identified by the appropriate PICA NIMSC and formalized by DMISA.

c. The PICA will be responsible for the repair (organically or contractually) of all items for which it has been assigned the depot level maintenance function. When the PICA provides support under NIMSCs 3, 4, or 8, depot level maintenance requirements will be negotiated with the SICA and accomplished under a formalized DMISA, as required.

d. The SICA service, when receiving support under NIMSC 3, 4, or 8, will negotiate a DMISA for depot level maintenance repair requirements, as required.

2-8. Disposal:

a. **Responsibilities:**

(1) The SICA will be responsible for determining quantities of nonconsumable items in excess of SICA requirements.

(2) The PICA will be the single agency responsible for determining quantities excess to DOD requirements.

(3) The PICA will be the only DOD component authorized to approve disposal of excess assets under its management cognizance.

b. **Procedures:**

(1) Excess reporting and responses between the SICA and PICA will be accomplished using procedures in DOD 4160.21-M.

(2) The SICA will report excess assets to the PICA.

(3) The PICA will determine if a requirement for the reported excess exists including advising other military users of the available excess. Upon confirmation of other service requirements for the excess, the PICA will provide disposition instructions to the SICA.

(4) The PICA will offer its excess assets to other military users before disposal action is taken.

Chapter 3

PHASE II ITEM PROCESSING

3-1. General. These policies and procedures will be used to select and review items for migration to NIMSC 5 or 6 and subsequent management under Phase II criteria, or for migration to NIMSC 8 and retention in Phase I. Phase II is the expansion of the Phase I implementation program whereby wholesale stock, store, and issue functions for affected items are assigned to a single manager for DOD wholesale financial and asset control. This assignment includes:

(a) A single DOD wholesale stock.

(b) Sole development of budgeting and funding of depot maintenance requirements.

(c) Single budgeting and funding of requirements to support wholesale stock.

(d) Responsibility for effecting credit exchange.

(e) Critical item management.

(f) Determination, budgeting and funding of DOD wholesale war reserve requirements.

3-2. Items Subject to Phase II Implementation:

a. Policy. All multiservice used national stock numbered nonconsumable items assigned to a PICA, with the exception of consistently managed end items of equipment and Navy air launched missile items managed under 8E cognizance symbol (generally FSG 14), are eligible for Phase II management. All consistently managed depot reparable components and all inconsistently managed items must be reviewed. Items currently recorded with NIMSC 5 or 6 within the SICA service are excluded from this review. These items are already under the Phase II management concept. Single used nonconsumable items will be reviewed upon item adoption by another service.

b. Procedures:

(1) The PICA is responsible for item selection and negotiating a review schedule with the SICAs. The PICA will provide a copy of negotiated schedules as well as any scheduling conflicts/problems encountered to service NIS focal points. The NIPC will resolve/schedule for review those items wherein ICPs are unable to negotiate firm schedules.

(2) First priority for review will be those items scheduled for interservice

repair on negotiated DMISAs and/or currently scheduled for purchase.

(3) The objective of item review is acceptance or development of a single procurement specification and a single depot repair specification by all service users of the item. Item reviews may be conducted either on an individual NSN basis or on a system/equipment basis. PICAs and SICAs will collaborate to review items on a system/equipment basis when such reviews will promote consistent PICA assignments and consistent NIMSC assignments for the involved items.

(4) The PICA will provide a review package, unless otherwise agreed to between PICA and SICA, consisting of the Certificate of Usability (appendix A); the PICA's procurement specifications; repair specifications; packaging specifications; and checklist (appendix E) to each recorded SICA. The SICA will complete review of the package and return the signed Certificate to the PICA within 120 days from the date of the PICA transmittal letter. Each SICA will sign and date the Certificate of Usability when it is in agreement with the specifications. In those instances where a SICA nonconcurs with the PICA specifications, the SICA will document detailed reasons for nonconcurrence and will request support under NIMSC 2 or NIMSC 8 as appropriate. Upon receipt, the PICA will attempt to resolve all differences. This action will be accomplished within 60 days from the date of the SICA transmittal letter. Failure to establish acceptable procurement and depot repair specifications between PICA and a SICA will result in the SICA retaining item management under Phase I criteria and continuing the existing depot maintenance arrangement. In these cases, NIMSC 8 will be assigned. If no DMISA exists, the PICA will assign NIMSC 2.

(5) SICAs will review PICA depot repair specification when SICA manages the item as consumable to determine if an item repaired under the PICA's repair specification, or an acceptable revision to the PICA repair specification, would satisfy SICA requirement. If a repaired PICA asset would not satisfy the SICA requirement, the SICA will continue to manage the item under Phase I criteria as NIMSC 2.

(6)   A secondary objective of the item procurement and depot repair specifications review is the establishment of consistent management application by all using services. Services managing the item as consumable will review depot repair specifications established by another using service to determine if unserviceable generations in the service managing as consumable should be subject to depot repair. If it is determined that such unserviceables should be repaired at the depot, the SICA will initiate action to change the management level coding to nonconsumable; the PICA will subsequently assign NIMSC 5. If it is determined that unserviceables should not be subject to depot repair, the PICA will assign NIMSC 2 or NIMSC 6 as appropriate.

(7)   Acceptance of a single procurement specification and a single depot repair specification by the PICA and at least one SICA will result in the item migrating to the PICA for management under Phase II criteria and the assignment of NIMSC 5. SICAs nonconcurring with the procurement and/or depot repair specification will continue to manage the item in accordance with support arrangements as reflected by that SICA's NIMSC. Justification for retention of wholesale management responsibilities by the nonconcurring SICAs rests with the nonconcurring SICAs.

(8)   A Certificate of Usability (appendix A) will be completed for each item wherein PICA and at least one SICA have concurred with both procurement and depot repair specifications. The Certificate of Usability will be signed by the service's designated representatives and is evidence that assets provided by the PICA will satisfy SICA requirements. The document will be kept in the item jacket/ folder until no longer applicable.

(9)   An effective transfer date will be assigned for each item for which a Certificate of Usability has been signed under the provisions of this regulation.

(10)   Contact points will be set up and made known by each ICP to process all management data information relating to the Phase II implementation.

(11)   When a service has a requirement to adopt an item previously assigned to a PICA, the adopting service will assign a comparable MLC to that established by the existing PICA to provide consistent management.

Chapter 4

LOGISTICS REASSIGNMENT (LR)

4-1. General:

a. The policies and procedures in this chapter are used to effect nonconsumable item Logistics Reassignment (LR) resulting from migrations from Phase I to Phase II made in accordance with chapter 3 of this regulation and chapter 6 DOD 4000.25-2-M, Military Standard Transaction Reporting and Accounting Procedures (MILSTRAP).

b. Financial policies and procedures and reporting requirements for LRs are given in Chapter 6 of this regulation.

c. To facilitate logistics reassignment, the LR process has been divided into three periods of time based upon the Effective Transfer Date (ETD). The periods are identified as pre-ETD, ETD, and post-ETD. The pre-ETD period starts on the date of final approval of the Certificate of Usability and ends at ETD. The ETD is established as the date that the NIMSC 5 or 6 activated in the Federal files and is the date of the LR. Post-ETD covers the period of time following ETD. DLSC has established the NIMSC as a dated data element. The PICA/SICAs will establish a mutually acceptable ETD not to exceed 180 days after final approval of the Certificate of Usability. Although the ETD is a specific point in time, for the purpose of this publication, any actions involving data requirements that reflect conditions as of the ETD will be discussed as if such actions took place on the ETD, even though they may have been taken immediately before or after the actual ETD. The specific events required to take place during LR are delineated under the appropriate period.

4-2. Policy:

a. The SICAs will be notified through DIDS whenever the PICA submits a change to the NIMSC. An NIMSC change to 5 or 6 from other than NIMSC 5 or 6 will identify an item subject to decapitalization/ capitalization action and Phase II management. The PICA will establish the effective date for NIMSC change which will also be used as the effective transfer date for logistics reassignment. This date will be the PICA/SICA negotiated date not to exceed 180 days beyond the date the transaction is input to the DLSC TIR. When a change in PICA assignment has been negotiated, the gaining PICA will input cataloging changes.

b. On items being logistically reassigned to a PICA, the SICA(s) will maintain stock level through the pre-ETD period at the stock levels that would have been maintained if the items were not going to be logistically reassigned.

c. A physical inventory of the on-hand wholesale assets will be performed within 150 days before ETD and inventory records reconciled as required.

d. The SICAs will establish retail and wholesale stock levels before ETD. All on-hand wholesale assets excess to total system retail requirements of the SICA will be decapitalized in place on ETD with the exception of those assets designated or held for specific program/projects within the services and those held in MILSTRAP condition codes G, H, J, K, L, M, and P. Condition code H and P materiel will never be decapitalized. SICAs are authorized to dispose of condition code H items and to complete reclamation of condition code P assets without reporting to the PICA, unless the PICA, due to a critical item support position, requests the SICA to report H and P condition asset availability.

(1) The SICA will attempt to reclassify condition code G, J, K, L, and SICA-held M condition material to an acceptable condition code prior to ETD. Condition code G, J, K, L and M materiel, upon transfer to an acceptable condition subsequent to ETD, will be decapitalized to the PICA unless held for specific SICA programs, projects or retail requirements.

(2) The SICA will attempt to reclassify to an acceptable condition code, assets located at another service DMISA site or at a commercial repair site prior to the ETD. Such materiel, upon converting to an acceptable condition code after ETD, will be decapitalized to the PICA unless held for specific SICA programs, projects or retail requirements.

e. The responsible contracting office of the SICA(s) will process to completion all uncompleted contracts covering items to be transferred. Indefinite delivery type contracts or multi-year contracts, where the remaining contract period exceeds 1 calendar year from the ETD, may be transferred subject to review and mutual agreement of the responsible contracting offices of the PICA/SICAs involved. Contract administration responsibility, not assigned to the Defense Contract Administration Service (DCAS), will remain with the contracts.

f. Decapitalized stocks will remain under the physical care and custody of the SICA service(s) storage site(s) where the materiel was decapitalized until it is issued, relocated, or disposed of at the direction of the PICA. Decapitalized stocks will be relocated when the requester (PICA or SICA) determines it is more economical or essential to physically consolidate or ship materiel to storage locations under the control of the PICA rather than to attrit the stocks in place. The transportation and accessorial costs for relocation of stocks for consolidation will be borne by the requester (PICA or SICA).

g. The PICA will, within 30 days of receipt of the consummation of the Certificate of Usability, input the appropriate NIMSC change (NIMSC 5 or 6) to the TIR maintained at DLSC. The effective date for NIMSC change is established as the ETD for LR and will be assigned according to paragraph 4-2a. The SICA service will establish internal procedures to ensure decapitalization of applicable wholesale assets on the ETD.

h. Upon SICA receiving notification from DLSC or from the PICA of the effective date of NIMSC change to 5 or 6, the SICA activity will validate the SICA source of supply (SOS) and initiate change, if appropriate, and ensure that all field units are advised and that decapitalization action, if required, is started.

i. Request for PICA reassignment will be made by use of the JLC Form 19 (Appendix F).

j. When a PICA service is no longer a user of the item, the PICA should negotiate reassignment to a SICA service. The major SICA service user should accept PICA responsibility. However, such responsibility should not be assumed until the item is in a supportable position. The PICA will not take action to delete its recording until the SICA confirms acceptance of PICA responsibilities. If the PICA has been assigned the depot maintenance, the PICA service MISMO will be notified so that the depot maintenance assignment can be reevaluated as necessary. If a service other than the original PICA has been assigned the depot maintenance, that service will continue providing the depot maintenance for all other users. If the SICA does not agree to become PICA, the existing recorded PICA must continue furnishing supply support including depot repair, if assigned, although not a user.

4-3. Procedures for Pre-ETD Period. The following actions will be taken during the pre-ETD period:

a. The SICA will make sure back orders have been validated according to DOD 4000.25-1-M (MILSTRIP) Materiel Obligation Validation (MOV) procedures prior to ETD.

b. The SICA will discontinue redistribution of wholesale stocks of those items assigned to a PICA 60 days before ETD.

c. The SICA will notify the PICA during the pre-ETD period of any item that is or may become in short supply (for example, less than minimum reserve/control level) so that mutually agreed-to corrective action can be taken.

d. The SICA will furnish management data, if requested by the PICA, such as: Price history, bidders list, requirements type contracts, industrial readiness information, and other purchase data. Based on coordination efforts between the PICA and SICA, a specified date will be set up to physically transfer these data. In addition, the SICA will furnish the PICA a Requirements Data Exchange Card (RDEC) (appendix C) not less than 90 days before ETD. An updated RDEC may be submitted, if appropriate, after initial submission. The SICA will also provide a JLC Form 15 (Asset Reporting)(appendix B) in lieu of the supply item control studies specified in chapter 6 of DOD 4000.25-2-M, Military Standard Transaction Reporting and Accounting Procedures (MILSTRAP) to reflect wholesale assets as of the submission date and project wholesale assets available on the ETD.

e. The PICA will review outstanding contracts, along with the applicable SICA, and determine if assets scheduled to be delivered to SICA wholesale storage points should be diverted to PICA storage activities.

f. If requested by the PICA, the SICA will start action approximately 45 days before the ETD to amend existing contracts/ purchase orders where feasible for items being transferred to provide for diversion of shipments of stock buy quantities into the storage depots of the PICA. The PICA will provide addresses of the shipping destinations to the SICA as appropriate.

g. The PICA will determine the number of assets required in the wholesale system and will use its parent service policies and procedures. The PICA will consider all SICA assets which will be made available from decapitalization actions. When the PICA determines that the total of the PICA wholesale assets and SICA decapitalized assets isn't sufficient to support new PICA wholesale levels, due to insufficiency of SICA decapitalized assets, the PICA will negotiate, on a case-by-case basis, with the applicable SICA to obtain required funds/assets for support. During such negotiations, decapitalized asset insufficiencies on one item will be offset to the extent that assets on the other items to be decapitalized on the same date reduce PICA procurement and/or repair requirements through the apportionment year.

h. In no case will the SICA be required to provide resources in a greater amount than it would have expended to satisfy its wholesale requirements had the SICA retained wholesale management responsibilities.

4-4. Procedures for ETD Period. The following will be accomplished:

a. The SICA service will transfer wholesale asset accountability to the PICA in the ETD in accordance with MILSTRAP.

b. All wholesale quantities in condition codes G, J, K, L and M which cannot be decapitalized on ETD will be reported by condition code to the PICA on JLC Form 15. The report should be submitted concurrently with decapitalization action. Negative reports are required. SICA on-hand assets may be used to fill SICA backorders prior to ETD. Due-ins won't be used to fill backorders after ETD. Validated outstanding backorders held by the SICA which cannot be satisfied from SICA retained assets will be sent to the PICA for action.

c. The PICA will assume the responsibility of wholesale supply support on ETD and will accept funded requisitions from all authorized requisitioners as of that date. SICA services which have not signed Certificate of Usability will obtain support in accordance with negotiated NIMSC.

4-5. Procedures for Post-ETD Period. The following will be accomplished:

a. The SICAs will process to completion all contracts executed by the service prior to the LR. Contract administration will also be performed by the SICA service except where the contract administration responsibility is assigned to another contract administration office.

b. The SICA will prepare and submit inventory adjustments to increase or decrease quantities previously transferred in accordance with the provisions of MILSTRAP.

c. Any wholesale stock (in acceptable condition codes) identified by the SICA within 1 year after ETD will be decapitalized to the PICA on an expedited basis. Some of the potential sources of these residual assets are:

(1) Stocks in transit.

(2) Stock previously suspended (condition codes J, K, G, and M).

(3) Stock previously under litigation (condition code L.

d. Stocks received from procurement will be decapitalized to the PICA regardless of when they are received.

e. Any wholesale stock identified by the SICA subsequent to the ETD plus 1 year will be reported to the PICA as excess in accordance with MILSTRIP.

f. The PICA will take action to issue, relocate, or dispose of wholesale materiel at SICA attrition sites (nonpermanent storage locations) after the ETD. This action will be taken by means of Materiel Release Orders (MROs) for issue or relocation action and by Disposal Release Orders (DROs) for disposal actions using MILSTRIP formats. Insofar as practicable, stocks held at attrition sites will be issued ahead of other stocks at other sites.

g. If requested by the PICA, the SICA will furnish price history, bidders' list, contractors' requirement type contracts, industrial readiness information, and other procurement data as specified in DOD 5010.12. These data are to be furnished within 30 days from the receipt of the request. If this date cannot be met, provide the available data and the date when the remaining data will be furnished within 30 days. The inclusion of this event in the post-ETD won't preclude the PICA from requesting these data during the pre-ETD period.

Chapter 5

SUPPLY OPERATIONS (NIMSC 5 OR 6)

5-1. General. Policies and procedures contained in this chapter support sustained operations following item migration and Phase II management, in the performance of Supply Operations, by the PICA and the SICA.

5-2. PICA Assignments:
  a. Policy. Nonconsumable items entering the DOD inventory will be assigned to a single military service for materiel management.
  b. Procedures:
    (1) Nonconsumable items entering the DOD inventory as replacement for items previously assigned to a PICA will be assigned to the PICA for the replaced item if or when the PICA adopts the replacing item.
    (2) Nonconsumable items entering the DOD inventory which are not replacements for currently established items in the DOD inventory and those new nonconsumable items which enter as replacements but are not adopted by the PICA, will be assigned to the introducing service. If items are identified as a result of joint provisioning action or a joint acquisition project, the designated executive service or the service assigned life cycle responsibility for the weapon system, subsystem or next higher assembly requiring the new item will be assigned as PICA on all multiservice used items. When items are peculiar to one service, PICA responsibility will be assigned to that service. In some instances, when agreed to by the services involved, PICA assignment may be made to a service which is not a user of the item. If mutual agreement for PICA assignment cannot be reached, the item, with supporting data, will be submitted to the applicable service's NIPC focal point for resolution.
    (3) In those instances where the MISMO decision is not received before the provisioning conference, PICA assignments should be recorded in the DLSC TIR with PICA NIMSC U and SICA NIMSC 9. These items will require review after receipt of depot repair assignment by the MISMO and processed as follows:
    (a) If the MISMO notification indicates no projected depot repair requirements, recommends contract repair, or if the PICA is the recommended organic repair activity, the PICA will negotiate with the SICA the required level of support and record the appropriate NIMSC in the DLSC TIR.
    (b) If the MISMO notification names a military service as the organic depot repair activity and that service is other than the PICA, the PICA must determine if item management responsibility should be transferred to that service. If the PICA concurs, the PICA will negotiate the transfer of PICA responsibilities to the appropriate service ICP. If the PICA has adequate justification for the retention of the PICA management responsibilities, with depot maintenance performed by a SICA, that justification will be forwarded to PICA service NIPC member for documentation. Appropriate cataloging action should then be taken, with the PICA NIMSC identifying the service actually performing depot maintenance. If the PICA service has adequate rationale for requiring a change to the depot maintenance assignment, that rationale will be sent to the PICA service MISMO for Joint service MISMO negotiation. After MISMO consideration or resolution, appropriate cataloging action will be directed.

5-3. Provisioning:
  a. Policy. For provisioning actions concerning multiservice used nonconsumables, the SICAs are to provide peculiar SICA requirements to the PICA and the PICA will collaborate with the SICAs to schedule joint provisioning actions whenever practicable. Particular emphasis is placed upon MIL-STD-1338 and use of uniform source, maintenance and recoverability (SMR) codes as prescribed by AR 700-82, OPNAVINST 4410-2, AFR 66-45, MCO 4400.120, DSAR 4100.6 and implementing instructions. In addition, PICA and SICA will strive to standardize maintenance plans and SMR codes for each nonconsumable. A coordinated plan for maintenance will be developed for each nonconsumable that describes repair/maintenance actions to be performed at each level of maintenance to ease the provisioning process. This is not to be interpreted as meaning that the plan for maintenance must be the same for each service; rather that each service strives to meet this common objective. Where standardization of procedures is not possible because of peculiar requirements based on differences in service roles and mission, each

using service will be required to document these differences.

   b. **Procedures:**

      (1) Each service will compute initial requirements as provided by DODI 4140.42. Whenever the adopting service establishes an MLC that is inconsistent with the MLC currently established by the PICA, the basis for the decision will be fully justified and documented.

      (2) The PICA will obtain an NSN and, if applicable, record SICA MOE Rule for assigned noncataloged items within 90 days of SICA request. The PICA will not register a SICA until a NIMSR is received from that SICA.

      (3) The PICA will negotiate a support date for each SICA for all new NSNs entering the supply system. The Materiel Support Date (MSD) will be annotated on the NIMSR that is returned to the SICA. Prior to the MSD, all requirements of the SICA must be processed to the PICA using MIPR, unless exceptions are provided by the PICA.

5-4. Item Adoption:
   a. **Policy:**

      (1) A service that has a requirement for and adopts a previously-established NSN nonconsumable item or establishes a requirement for a noncataloged item during joint provisioning will negotiate item support from the assigned PICA. The SICA services will normally assign SMR codes compatible with those assigned by the PICA which will result in consistent management level coding.

      (2) The PICA must provide wholesale stock, store, and issue functions for requesting SICAs if the PICA maintains wholesale stock in support of its own service activities. The PICA will not be obligated to provide such support prior to a mutually-acceptable MSD negotiated between the PICA and each SICA.

      (3) When a service has a requirement to adopt an item previously assigned to a PICA the adopting service should assign a comparable MLC to that established by the existing PICA to provide consistent management.

   b. **Procedures:**

      (1) The PICA/SICA shall negotiate a mutually-acceptable MSD upon which the PICA must provide wholesale stock, store and issue functions to the SICA. This will be accomplished by use of the NIMSR (appendix D).

      (2) The SICAs will provide the PICA with any additional data required by the PICA to ensure support.

      (3) The PICA will input SICA MOE rule and NIMSC within 30 days after receipt of SICA adopt request.

      (4) The SICAs will insure that SICA CMD is recorded in the DLSC files in accordance with DOD 4100.39-M.

5-5. Item Stockage:
   a. **Policy.** The PICA, in coordination with involved SICAs, is responsible for determining if an item should be stocked at the wholesale level. The PICA will not designate a Phase II (NIMSC 5) item as nonstocked (i.e. AAC J) without the concurrence of the SICA.

   b. **Procedures:**

      (1) The PICA will apply its parent service policy in determining if new items, assigned to the PICA, should be stocked or nonstocked. Stockage decisions will be recorded in the DLSC TIR according to DIDS procedures.

      (2) The PICA's item stockage decision for multiservice used nonconsumable items, recorded in the DLSC TIR, is reflected by the PICA's assigned acquisition advice code. A PICA will not change an item's stockage status from stocked to nonstocked without obtaining SICA service coordination. If a SICA service determines that wholesale stocks must be maintained in order to provide timely resupply to its operational forces on items that the PICA has recommended be converted from stocked to nonstocked status, the PICA will continue to maintain wholesale stock. As an alternative, the PICA may negotiate transfer of PICA management to the SICA service requiring the maintenance of wholesale stock.

5-6. Cataloging:
   a. **Policy:**

      (1) Cataloging actions will be in accordance with DOD 4100.39M. The PICA will be the single submitter cataloger, except for SICA-peculiar CMD. SICA proposed changes to item data, other than SICA CMD, will be submitted to the PICA for processing. The PICA will:

      (a) Review and determine appropriate actions.

      (b) Collaborate (as required by DOD 4100.39-M, DIDS Procedures Manual) with recorded users.

      (c) Resolve all conflicts from collaboration prior to sending to DLSC.

      (d) Send the coordinated action to DLSC.

(2) The DLSC will process add/change/-delete actions applicable to segments of the DLSC TIR only when received from the PICA except for Segment H, CMD, SICA-peculiar data.

(a) The PICA will be uniquely identified by a PICA MOE Rule with a LOA of 22. A valid alpha NIMSC is mandatory.

(b) The SICA will be uniquely identified by a SICA MOE Rule with a LOA of 8D. A valid numeric NIMSC is mandatory.

b. **Procedures:**

(1) For a new nonconsumable items entering the system, the service introducing the item (or the service designated in joint provisioning) will request NSN assignment and will be recorded in the DLSC TIR with the appropriate PICA MOE Rule and LOA 22.

(2) When another service wants to adopt an established nonconsumable NSN, that service will submit a NIMSR to the recorded PICA. The PICA will submit an adopt transaction to DLSC reflecting the SICA MOE Rule and proposed NIMSC from the NIMSR or the PICA/SICA collaborated changes thereto.

(3) When a SICA service desires a NIMSC change, a JLC form 19 (PICA/SICA Management Level Change and/or Reassignment Request)(appendix F) must be forwarded to the PICA service ICP for concurrence and submission to DLSC by the PICA. Requests for NIMSC changes are not sent by the SICA service directly to DLSC for action. The NIMSC changes will be effective in accordance with DOD 4100.39-M.

(4) Sica (LOA_8D) MOE rule changes will be sent to the PICA for input to DLSC.

(5) Catalog Management Data:

(a) SICA (LOA-8D) activities reflecting NIMSC of 1 through 5 or 8 and 9 will show the SICA activity as SOS. The AAC will be compatible with the SICA SOS and requisition guides.

(b) SICA (LOA-8D) activities reflecting a NIMSC 6 will reflect the PICA SOS and AAC subject to DOD 4100.39-M

(c) PICA CMD update for other than SICA-peculiar data and the SOS/AAC correlation referenced above will automatically update corresponding SICA CMD elements.

5-7. Requirements Computation/Methodology:

a. **Policy.** The PICA will use the requirements, procedures, and methodology of its parent service. Item demand projections provided on the RDEC provided by the SICA will be considered in computing wholesale stock requirements. The SICA will compute retail requirements to provide the PICA with SICA-projected requisitioning requirements, projected unserviceable returns, and Other War Reserve Materiel Requirements (OWRMR).

b. **Procedures:**

(1) SICA will use the RDEC to provide PICA with projected materiel requirements. SICA will provide annually projected materiel requirements to the PICA for every NIMSC 5 item by 1 February of each year. SICA may update these projections, on an item-by-item basis, at any time before the next annual submission.

(2) Effective with the ETD, all support to another SICA service for a nonconsumable item under the terms of an existing Wholesale Interservice Supply Support Agreement (WISSA) is terminated and support will be provided under the terms of this regulation. Budget/funding responsibilities are identified in Chapter 6.

5-8. Management Level Code (MLC) Changes and PICA/SICA Reassignment Requests:

a. **Policy:**

(1) Proposed changes to management techniques (nonconsumable to consumable or consumable to nonconsumable) will not be made by the PICA or SICA without prior coordination with all other registered users. PICA/SICA proposed changes to management techniques will be submitted with supporting rationale on JLC Form 19.

(2) Final determination of management technique applied to an individual item rests with each using service.

b. **Procedure:**

(1) PICA-initiated proposed MLC changes which would impact on SICA service will be provided to applicable SICA services by Part I, JLC Form 19, with supporting rationale. SICA initiated proposed Management Level Code (MLC) changes will be provided to PICA by Part I JLC Form 19 with supporting rationale for the change. PICA will provide these data to other SICA when applicable.

(2) The SICA receiving proposed MLC changes will review the rationale provided to determine if their MLC should also be changed. Response will be provided within 120 days by completing Part II of the JLC of the Form 19 received from the PICA.

(3) The PICA assignment for items currently managed as consistent consumables; that is, an IMM is assigned, for items

converted to nonconsumables as a result of an MLC change, will be accomplished as follows:

(a) If the current manager is an IMM, the DLSC TIR will be updated by the IMM or gaining Inventory Manager with the appropriate PICA/SICA MOE/LOA rules to reflect nonconsumable item management. Any change to materiel management assignment must be through negotiation of parties involved prior to DLSC update. If the change in management results in an inconsistent management situation under Phase I procedures, existing wholesale inventories will be reallocated on a basis which recognizes the new division of wholesale support responsibilities for the item. Normally, such reconstitution of a SICA wholesale inventory will be based on relative installed item populations.

(b) If the current manager is a Commodity Integrated Materiel Manager (CIMM), the military service changing the item to a nonconsumable will notify all other military users of proposed action to obtain materiel management responsibilities from the CIMM. The service requesting the return action will assume PICA assignment and must provide the same degree of logistics support to all users as previously provided by the CIMM until degree of support has been negotiated by the PICA/SICA.

(4) Management level changes which result in consistently managed consumables will be processed according to DOD 4140.26-M.

(5) If an MLC change effects or alters the MISMO maintenance assignment, the PICA will advise its service MISMO within 30 days for Joint MISMO resolution. The MISMO resolution will be provided within 90 days of the request. The PICA will then take cataloging action to reflect the latest MISMO maintenance decision.

5-9. Distribution Systems/Levels:

a. **General.** Within distribution systems/levels, the general procedures outlined below concern three areas:

(1) Decapitalization/ capitalization action.

(2) Requisition processing by the PICA.

(3) Physical inventory.

b. **Policy:**

(1) The overall system level of supply (wholesale requirements objectives) will be as determined by the PICA. Individual service activity retail levels will be as determined by the SICA service.

(2) Each SICA service will establish /maintain separate service accounts at each holding activity with wholesale stock which was decapitalized and is being maintained for the PICA.

(3) Distribution/redistribution of wholesale assets will be made only by direction of the PICA.

(4) Physical relocation of stocks from attrition sites (SICA service storage sites) will be according to paragraph 4-2f.

(5) Stocks may be positioned by the PICA as determined by the emerging overall demand pattern. This may include positioning wholesale stocks at an activity of another DOD component subject to negotiation with the other DOD component.

c. **Procedures/Methods:**

(1) Decapitalization/ Capitalization Action:

(a) Upon establishment of ETD, the SICA service will determine the quantity of stock to be retained in the SICA's retail inventory. The remaining quantity of materiel will be decapitalized in place on ETD and reported to to the PICA in accordance with MILSTRAP.

(b) The SICA service will establish appropriate attrition records and will issue materiel transferred by LR upon receipt of appropriate MILSTRIP documentation from the PICA. The SICA service will submit appropriate MILSTRIP/ MILSTRAP reports to the PICA.

(2) **Requisition Processing:**

(a) SICA service activities will submit requisitions to the appropriate SOS for the PICA-managed nonconsumables. All documents will be as prescribed by MILSTRIP.

(b) Requisitions will be processed in accordance with paragraph 5-10. All assets visible to the PICA and considered as wholesale assets by the PICA in filling his own service requisitions will be made available on an equal basis for all service requisitions per paragraph 5-11.

(c) Attrition stocks held in SICA storage sites will normally be issued ahead of stock located at other sites.

(d) Requisitions from nonregistered users should be honored if the PICA service support won't be jeopardized.

(3) Physical Inventory:

(a) Physical inventories will be conducted in accordance with DODI 4140.35.

(b) Physical inventory requests and results will be transmitted between the PICA and the SICA service attrition sites as specified in MILSTRAP.

5-10. Requisitioning Channels:

a. **Policy.** Use the standard MILSTRAP system for requisitioning. DAAS will maintain source of supply by item as directed by the individual service.

b. **Procedures/Methods:**

(1) The flow of requisitions within a given service will continue to be prescribed by that particular service; however, requisitions for NIMSC 5 items will flow from SICA activities via the SICA ICP for funding, prioritization, and requisition control purposes. The SICA will transmit these requirements ia DAAS to the PICA. Funded requisitions for NIMSC 6 items will be submitted by the SICA requiring activities directly to the PICA through DAAS.

(2) All MILSTRIP transaction applicable to SICA NIMSC 5 items will be provided to the SICA via DAAS consistent with assigned Media and Status Codes (Transaction Position 7) and Distribution Codes (Transaction Position 54) entries.

5-11. Priority Application/Asset Release.

a. **Policy.** Use the Uniform Materiel Movement and Issue Priority System (UMMIPS) to assign the appropriate Issue Priority Designator (IPD) to requisitions. Requisitions will be filled from PICA wholesale stocks in accordance with MILSTRIP procedures without regard to the service affiliation of the requisitioning activity. Control levels and maximum release quantities for each item will be established by the PICA.

b. **Procedures.** The PICA will process requisitions in accordance with the assigned UM-MIPS IPDs and time standards. Requisitions will be filled in the sequence established by MILSTRIP. PICA will go to the same depth of wholesale assets in satisfying all services' requisitions. The PICA performing maximum release quantity checks will apply this check to all services' requisitions. When quantities requested exceed the maximum release quantity established by the PICA, the customer will be advised of the action taken in accordance with MILSTRIP.

5-12. Critical Item Management:

a. **General.** A critical item is an essential item which is in short supply or expected to be in short supply for an extended period and has been designated critical by the PICA.

b. **Policy.** Each PICA/SICA will employ its own critical item management program.

c. **Procedures:**

(1) The PICA will ensure its own service critical item procedures contain, as a minimum, physical inventory guidelines, expedited acquisition and depot repair, handling and shipping routines, and special asset release techniques.

(2) The criteria for establishment/disestablishment of critical items will be that currently used by the PICA. Recommendations from the SICA to designate an item as critical will be considered by the PICA. Issue restrictions will be placed on items by the PICA as soon as they are designated critical. Every effort will be made by the PICA to ensure equitable allocation and distribution of assets. Assets will be applied to requirements according to paragraph 5-11.

(3) PICAs/SICAs will use rapid means of communication for reporting of assets of designated critical items.

5-13. War Reserve (Mobilization Reserve Materiel Requirements):

a. **Policy:**

(1) War Reserve Materiel Requirements. Each SICA will be responsible for providing its OWRMR to the PICA. The PICA will consolidate all requirements to arrive at the total wholesale war reserve materiel requirement. The total wholesale war reserve requirement will be offset through industrial preparedness measures by the PICA. Inventory management responsibilities for the wholesale requirement will be accomplished by the PICA.

(2) Prepositioned War Reserve Requirements. The computation and inventory management of the prepositioned war reserve requirement/ prepositioned war reserve stock will be the responsibility of each individual service.

b. **Procedures:**

(1) War Reserve Materiel Requirements.

(a) Each service will compute a war reserve materiel requirement for nonconsumable item requirements under the management of another service. The prepositioned war reserve requirement will be subtracted from the war reserve materiel requirement and the difference (OWRMR) forwarded to the PICA through the use of RDEC cards. The PICA will consolidate the requirements of each service to arrive at the total wholesale requirement.

(b)   The PICA will ensure that all wholesale war reserve assets are protected/reserved and that issuance to satisfy peacetime requirements is limited to those conditions authorized by DOD directives. Any issues made to satisfy a peacetime requirement will be accordingly reconstituted.

(c)   The PICA will ensure that any funds made available through reinvestment procedures are applied to war reserve materiel requirement deficits in the wholesale inventory.

(2)   Prepositioned War Reserve Requirement. Each service will compute the prepositioned war reserve requirement and include the requirement in applicable budgets. Prepositioned war reserve stock will be procured by the PICA upon receipt of an MIPR and delivered to the SICA accordingly. When the PICA determines that assets to fill a prepositioned war reserve requirement are in excess of the AFAO, the PICA will issue the assets free of charge.

5-14.   Inactive Items:
    a.   Policy. The PICA will identify/select potentially inactive items for possible elimination from the supply system and the Federal Catalog in accordance with DOD 4140.32-M, Defense Inactive Item Program.

    b.   Procedures:
        (1)   The PICA identifies and refers inactive items to registered users (SICAs) for review and a delete/retain decision in accordance with procedures outlined in DOD 4140.32-M.

        (2)   The SICAs will review the recommended inactive items for future potential use by the SICA and will coordinate with the International Logistics Center Office, as appropriate, and provide the PICA with the SICA's recommendation for retention/deletion.

        (3)   Items will not be deleted without the concurrence of all SICAs.

5-15.   International Logistics. Policies and procedures will be published when available.

5-16.   Standardization:
    a.   General. Standardization is implemented primarily through the use of federal and military specifications, standards, and handbooks listed in the Department of Defense Index of Specifications and Standards.

    b.   Policy. The PICA will be the coordinating authority for standardization actions affecting their assigned item. This will not change the existing DOD Standardization Assignee.

    c.   Procedures:
        (1)   The PICA, as the coordinating authority, will use the procedures defined in DOD 4120.3-M.

        (2)   The PICA will communicate with the Standardization Assignee Activity for the FSC involved or with the preparing activity of standardization documents under the following conditions.

        (a)   When a standardization document for multiservice used items is needed and does not exist.

        (b)   When standardization documents for multiservice nonconsumable items exist but are found to be inadequate.

        (3)   The PICA will communicate with the preparing activity of the documents involved with recommendations for the changes needed to existing documents. Communication may be made by use of DD Form 1426, Standardization Document Improvement Proposal, which is attached to each military specification.

        (4)   The PICA will provide all of the data in its file to the Standardization Assignee in accordance with the DOD 4120.3-M.

        (5)   The PICA will, through its departmental standardization activity, cause entry into the DOD Index of Specifications and Standards to reflect the degree of interest; i.e., preparer, custodian, and/or review activity.

5-17.   Reclamation.
    a.   Policy:
        (1)   Nonconsumable items to be reclaimed from aircraft/missiles/end items of equipment will be on direction of the PICA.

        (2)   The PICA manager will be responsible for identification of and assurance that their requirements are included on save lists for programmed reclamation at the Aerospace Maintenance and Regeneration Center (AMARC), Tuscon, Arizona.

        (3)   All services should be notified prior to nonprogrammed reclamation action so that PICA requirements may be included for save list recovery. PICA items must identified to the owning service system manager within 2 weeks of receipt of notification of nonprogrammed reclamation action. Nonprogrammed save lists will be assumed to be valid for 1 year from date of preparation, but the reclaiming manger

will notify all other participants prior to each new reclamation action. Participants will revalidate, add or delete items, and respond to the reclaiming activity within two weeks of each notification.

(4) If the PICA has advised the SICA that a nonconsumable item held by the SICA is excess and should be processed for disposal, then the SICA activity may reclaim for required components. The component breakdown of the item should be screened and if there are other service users of the components, they should be notified of the reclamation potential for their items. Screening and notification as above should also be accomplished when the PICA is reclaiming its own excess items.

b. **Procedures.** The procedures contained in DOD 4160.21-M will be used.

5-18. **Priority Removal.** When the SICA has a priority requirement and is aware that the item could be made available through priority removal, they will advise the PICA and, if priority removal criteria of the owning service are met, the PICA will request removal with direct shipment to the SICA activity and fund for the reclamation.

5-19. **Disposal.** The PICA will be the single DOD activity responsible for authorizing disposal of excess nonconsumable items under its cognizance. The procedures contained in DOD 4160.21-M will be used to effect disposal.

5-20. **Procurement:**

a. **Policy.** The PICA will be responsible for the acquisition of all assigned items. The PICA will not designate an item for local purchase (i.e. AAC L) without the concurrence of the SICA.

For items designated by the PICA for local purchase, the PICA will be responsible for effecting procurement action when requested by SICA activities due to SICA's inability to procure the item.

b. **Procedures:**

(1) The PICA will:

(a) Initiate procurement of assigned items in accordance with the FAR and parent service acquisition procedures.

(b) Provide written authorization for the SICA to initiate appropriate procurement action except for items designated for local purchase by AACL.

(c) Provide SICA with expected delivery dates when procurement is in support of SICA's MIPR.

(d) Administer the priorities and allocation authority in the purchase of assigned items through established channels in accordance with DODI 4400.1, Department of Defense Priorities and Allocations.

(e) Request and consolidate any available procurement source and pricing information from all other service users prior to initiating new procurements.

(2) The SICA will assure that PICA centrally procured items are not purchased by requiring activities under their control except when authorized by the PICA. In cases of emergency requirements, the purchase action will be limited to immediate use quantity. When emergency or PICA authorized purchases are made, one copy of the contractual instrument, plus any available source and pricing information, should be forwarded promptly to the appropriate PICA.

CHAPTER 6

PHASE II FINANCIAL MANAGEMENT (NIMSC 5 AND 6)

6-1. General. This chapter prescribes the policies and procedures for use in implementing and executing financial management for nonconsumable items where the PICA accomplishes wholesale stockage, storage and issue (NIMSC 5).

6-2. Scope. These policies and procedures apply to the activities of the Army, Navy, Air Force, and Marine Corps involved in financial operations/budgeting and funding for the logistics support of system/ equipment programs.

6-3. Policy:
a. Financial management of NIMSC 5 nonconsumable items is predicated on a fully reimbursable system whereby all issues from PICA wholesale stocks to the SICA will be reimbursable (billed at the standard price). Credit (65 percent of the standard price) will be allowed the SICA for all unserviceable NIMSC 5 assets received by the PICA when a replacement requisition has been submitted. Such credit will be applied when the unserviceable asset is received by the PICA. Credit will not be allowed for unserviceable returns when a replacement requisition has not been submitted.

b. The PICA will provide the operational resources for assigned logistics functions, including the funding for wholesale inventories, in accordance with DOD policies. The PICA will budget and fund for the net worldwide wholesale supply support requirements, DOD depot maintenance/overhaul requirements in support of reparable returns, washouts and PICA retail requirements. In cases where joint agreements result in a service being assigned as PICA for items it does not use, the PICA will carry out these same budgetary responsibilities.

c. Each service will be responsible for budgeting and funding the procurement lead time for protectable prepositioned war reserve requirements, initial provisioning/ outfittings (i.e., initial spares support list) requirements and follow-on provisioning/outfittings (follow-on spares support list) requirements. These requirements are considered retail requirements.

d. Reimbursement by the SICA for items procured from the PICA will be processed to the PICA by means of a MIPR or MILSTRIP requisition, as appropriate.

e. Serviceable items generated as excess within the SICA retail system will be offered to the PICA under current DOD prescribed material returns procedures.

f. No administrative or other general charges will be made by the PICA on issues, sales or transfers of material to a SICA.

g. Each SICA will be required to reimburse the PICA for support of SICA retail requirements to be requisitioned from the PICA wholesale system, including Foreign Military Sales, Security Assistance Program and Grant Aid and increases to such stocks.

h. Other billing techniques, such as charging the intraservice unit the net price initially, are permitted. This or other billing techniques may be adopted between two services if mutually agreed upon.

6-4. Specific Provisions:
a. **Budgeting and Funding:**
(1) The PICA will budget and fund for the recurring wholesale stockage levels to meet the SICA net replenishment requirements and for the overall depot maintenance overhaul requirements for projected reparable returns including depot condemnations. Budget documentation will differentiate between PICA and SICA requirements by service.

(2) The SICA will budget and fund recurring and nonrecurring retail stock requirements.

(3) The SICA will budget and fund nonrecurring requirements for all SICA protectable prepositioned war reserve requirements, prestocked war reserve requirements, initial provisioning/ outfitting (initial spares support list) requirements and follow-on provisioning/ outfitting (follow-on spares support list) requirements.

(4) The SICA will furnish a completed MIPR or funded MILSTRIP requisition, as determined by the PICA, for initial stock and unprogrammed requirements. A clear identification of priorities and need dates must be provided on each MIPR. Funding provided by MIPR will be subject to renegotiation, as necessary, to finance revised costs and/or additional costs incurred by the PICA for fulfilling requirements of the SICA. Increases, decreases, or other changes in fund authorization

will be effected by issuing of amendments to the funding documents.

(5) The PICA will provide a status report at least semiannually on all MIPRs submitted by each SICA. This report will be due 1 October and 1 April of each fiscal year.

(6) MILSTRIP requisitions will contain appropriate fund and signal codes for subsequent billing/crediting action on both initial stocking requirements and replenishment requisitions.

b. **Billing and Accounting:**

(1) Billings will be prepared by the PICA and submitted to the paying office in accordance with DODI 7420.12, DOD 4000.25-1M (MILSTRIP), and DOD 4000.25-7M (military standard billing system), as appropriate.

(2) Billings will be submitted monthly. Each bill will be on a net basis and will include complete documentation on all reimbursable issues and creditable returns (i.e., all unserviceable reparables returned when associated with a stock replacement requisition). As a minimum, documentation will include:

(a) National stock number.

(b) Reimbursable issues.

(c) Requisition number-shipping document number.

(d) Unserviceable receipts by document number.

(e) Creditable serviceable receipts by document number.

(f) Quantity-creditable receipt.

(g) Unit of issue.

(h) Extended price-reimbursable issue credit allowance.

(i) Net difference-debit/credit.

(3) All serviceable nonconsumable items, issued by the PICA to the SICA will be on a reimbursable basis and will be billed at 100 percent of standard price. For stock replacement requisitions, the SICA will receive a net credit of the difference between the standard price and actual experienced repair cost for all unserviceable assets returned to the PICA. Where actual repair costs are not available, a percent credit (65%) will be allowed which reflects the PICA's dollar weighted average repair cost for SICA items. Exceptions to this procedure may be adopted between two services if mutually agreed upon.

(4) Transportation costs incurred for shipment of material from the PICA to the SICA will be borne by the PICA service. Transportation costs incurred relative to the return of unserviceable or serviceable reparables by the SICA to the PICA will be borne by the SICA service.

(5) Reimbursement of sales to International Logistics Programs (including Military Assistance, Grant Aid, and Foreign Military Sales Cooperative Logistics Supply Support Arrangement transactions) will be in accordance with DODD 7290.1 and DOD 7290.3-M.

6-5. Decapitalization:

a. Decapitalization of on-hand wholesale assets in losing appropriation financed accounts and capitalization in the gaining accounts will be on a nonreimbursable basis for items to be supported under NIMSC 5.

b. After decapitalization, returns and credit policy for excess serviceable and economically reparable material will be in accordance with 6-4b(3).

c. Wholesale inventory pricing to the gaining service/PICA will be in accordance with the following:

(1) Items will be decapitalized in-place by the losing activity (SICA) and capitalized by the gaining activity (PICA) at the price recorded in the CMD record.

(2) The transfer unit price will be reflected in the transfer documents processed in accordance with MILSTRAP.

(3) Changes in prices will be held to a minimum to reduce inventory repricing and accounting at time of transfer.

(4) The gaining service (PICA) will not normally adjust prices of transferred items until the time of new procurement.

d. The SICA will provide operational resources in support of items transferred to a PICA until such attrition stock are issued or relocated from SICA locations.

e. Financial management responsibility/accountability for wholesale inventories of an item will be assumed by the PICA on the ETD. The SICAs have funding responsibility for clearing the existing pipelines, unless directed otherwise by the PICA.

f. The SICA will fund the following costs incidental to decapitalization:

(1) Continuation of procurement actions (contracts, purchase requests, and recommended buy quantity), unless otherwise requested by the PICA.

(2) Restoration costs of unserviceable material restored prior to ETD.

(3) Litigation/termination costs.

(4) Costs of first destination transportation for undelivered orders at time of transfer.

(5) Relocation costs (warehousing services and transportation) incidental to a SICA-requested movement of decapitalized stock from a SICA to a PICA designated storage site, unless otherwise negotiated.

g. The PICA will fund the following costs incidental to decapitalization:

(1) Transportation costs for material movements directed by the PICA other than those covered in subparagraph f(4) and (5) above.

(2) Repacking and repacking costs due to a PICA directed change in unit of issue/measure.

(3) Restoration costs for material capitalizated in an unserviceable condition and subsequently scheduled for restoration by the PICA.

h. Required adjustments to the budgeting and funding programs of the losing and gaining DOD components will be the responsibility of each service.

6-6. Impact of Office of the Secretary of Defense (OSD) Imposed Funding Constraints on PICA Support of SICA Requirements:

a. The PICA is required to notify the SICA when significant OSD budget reductions to the PICA procurement or repair funding are made and when such reductions may adversely impact support of SICA requirements.

b. In addition, the PICA will ensure that SICA service requirements are equitably supported based on Force Activity Designators (FAD) cited on SICA requisitions.

Chapter 7

PRICING

7-1. General. Pricing policies and procedures here apply to financial management, accounting, and reimbursement for integrated materiel within the PICA mission assignment.

7-2. Policy. The PICA will establish and maintain standard prices for centrally managed/depot reparable components in accordance with pricing policies of DODD 7200.7, Accounting and Pricing for Materiel Financed by Procurement Appropriations for Military Functions.

7-3. Procedures:

a. **General.** For inventory accounting purposes, each centrally managed national stock numbered depot component will have a single standard price regardless of the condition of the item. For reimbursement/ credit exchange purposes, the same standard price will be used except where price reductions are authorized and employed in accordance with DODD 7200.7.

b. **Composition of Standard Prices.** The standard price for each item will include the following elements:

(1) The current market or production cost of the item at time the price is established.

(2) A surcharge to cover authorized transportation costs as set forth in DODD 7200.7.

c. **Rounding Off Standard Prices.** Standard prices will be rounded off for all items with a minimum distortion of dollar data.

d. **Review and Revision of Standard Prices.** Standard prices shall be subject, but not limited, to review annually. Interim and annual reviews shall be accomplished for items for which a representative procurement has been made during the current year, where pricing errors are obvious, and in other instances deemed desirable by the PICA. Revised prices will be issued in accordance with DOD 4100.39-M.

Chapter 8

TECHNICAL SUPPORT

8-1. General. This chapter defines the procedures for communicating and executing configuration management, data management, maintenance work specifications, maintenance engineering, quality assurance and modification plans across service lines for nonconsumable items. The procedures in this chapter have been aligned with policy set forth in DODI 5010.19, DOD Configuration Management Program, and have augmented or expanded that policy, where necessary, to define the interrelationships and actions required between the involved military services, and to establish the communications channels for taking those actions. The concepts provided should enable the services to reduce proliferation of items and maximize standardization.

8-2. Scope:

a. These procedures apply to those multiservice used nonconsumable items where a single military service is designated as a PICA and one or more services are designated as a SICA. These procedures also apply to inconsistently managed items.

b. The policies and procedures of the Standard Integrated Support Management Systems (SISMS), AFLCR/AFSCR 800-24/ DARCOM-R 700-97/NAVMATINST 4000.38/MCO P4110.1A apply to this chapter except as modified or expanded here. For consistency, every effort will be made to establish the same service that is the executive service for a system as the PICA for the nonconsumable items. If a PICA assignment has been made to a service other than the designated executive service, the PICA will acquire necessary support by coordination with the executive service.

8-3. Responsibilities. The military service assigned as the executive service is responsible for the coordinated development and updating of management plans and actions to meet system life cycle requirements of all services, which include: acquisition, engineering, production, configuration management, quality assurance, product improvement, publications, provisioning, supply support, depot level maintenance training and support equipment, depot maintenance/ overhaul, testing, technical data, and field engineering services, packaging handling storage transportability (PHST)

and transportation. Each PICA is responsible for these actions for their individual items and must provide pertinent information to the executive service.

8-4. Procedures. The executive service will be responsible for developing and managing the Integrated Logistic Support process as set forth in DODD 5000.39 to ensure the timely, economical, and effective acquisition and positioning of technical and management logistics resources to meet the requirements of all using services. Particular emphasis will be placed upon those aspects impacting the system engineering process including appropriate support to program managers. Special attention will be placed upon standard technical documentation, coordination of maintenance plans, provisioning guidance and documentation, and technical manuals and data programs.

a. **Support Equipment.** When the PICA is the repair activity, the PICA will be solely responsible for design, funding, selection, acquisition, and modifications for peculiar support equipment required for depot repair of PICA assigned items. When support equipment qualify as a DMI candidate, OPNAVINST 4790.14, AMC R-750-10, AFLCR/AFSCR 800-30, MCO P4790.10A, Logistics Depot Maintenance Interservice Program procedures will be used for the JPCG-DMI SOR assignment. Where Automatic Test Equipment (ATE) is contemplated as the support equipment, DODD 5000.29 outlines considerations on computer resources which must be made by the appropriate PICA/SICA ATE manager.

b. **Government Furnished Equipment (GFE).** The user services will place particular emphasis on the early and orderly break out of GFE and initiate actions to procure nonconsumable items as GFE.

c. **Packaging, Handling, Shipping and Transportability (PHST).** The PICA will exercise management responsibility for PHST and related data for all NIMSC 5 and 6 items and make sure all users' PHST requirements are accommodated. The SICA will advise the PICA of any PHST requirements peculiar to SICA operations. The PICA will make known any required packaging and transportation instructions concerning retrograde materiel.

d. Facilities Determination and Planning. The service assigned depot maintenance responsibility is responsible for facility engineering, planning, and acquisition in support of depot maintenance. Each user service is responsible for facility engineering, planning and acquisition below the depot level. Those depot maintenance facility requirements qualifying as a New Start should be reviewed and approved in accordance with procedures established by the MISMOs.

e. Contractor Engineering and Technical Services (CETS). The PICA is responsible for the total CETS required in support of multiservice used nonconsumables with particular emphasis upon requirements in support of the depot and SICA operational needs. The SICA will make sure SICA requirements are provided to the PICA, along with funding and approval as required.

f. Interservice Depot Maintenance. In those instances where the PICA requires depot maintenance support from another military service, or the SICAs requires depot maintenance aid from the PICA, the disciplines and provisions of AFLC/AFSC 800-24/DARCOM-R 700-97/NAVMATINST 4000.38/ MCO P4110.1A will be used. The PICA, when requesting depot maintenance support from another service, will make sure the depot work specifications are compatible with all services' operational needs and will coordinate such specifications with involved SICAs if a Certificate of Usability has not been executed for the item.

g. Configuration Management. Configuration management will be addressed in all phases of the life cycle of nonconsumable items including design, development, production, deployment and operational phases.

(1) The cognizant configuration/ engineering management organizational element in the SICA service will be identified and recorded in block 29 of the NIMSR when the NIMSR is initiated. Likewise, the PICA will identify and record the PICA service configuration and engineering management organizational element in block 29 of the NIMSR when responding to the NIMSR. Direct liaison between the configuration and engineering management activities is encouraged. However, it is emphasized that the materiel management activities as identified in block 1 and 19 of the NIMSR should be apprised of any actions taken regarding configuration changes.

(2) The PICA will establish configuration item baselines, as appropriate, for multiservice used nonconsumables with a SICA NIMSC of 5 or 6. Required configuration status accounting will be coordinated to meet the needs of the involved services. Any SICA proposed configuration changes will be coordinated with the original PICA.

(3) The early distribution of materiel deficiency data, in accordance with DLAR 4155.24/AR 702-7/NAVMATINST 4855.8B/ AFR 74-6/MCO 4855.5B and authorized supplements thereto, to all user services and the coordination of corrective actions between the involved services, is essential to successful configuration management. Field units will submit deficiency reports to their respective service focal points. The service focal points will distribute the deficiency data to all user services configuration and engineering management elements as designated in the NIMSR. Responses to deficiency reports are required of all user services.

(4) If it is jointly determined that further investigative action is required, the PICA will arrange either organic or contractor engineering services. The PICA will make sure contracts for investigation, with request for Engineering Change Proposals (ECPs) prepared in accordance with DOD-STD 480 or MIL-STD 481, provide for simultaneous release of ECPs to all user services. Each involved service opting for investigative action will be responsible for a pro rata share of the cost, based upon the number of installed units. The PICA will negotiate these shared costs.

(5) Each requiring service will process engineering changes through internal Configuration Control Boards (CCB) to establish a service position prior to submission to the PICA. Any additional coordination will be established as required, between the PICA and SICAs to effect implementation. This will include validation of the engineering change proposal (ECP) by the PICA cognizant production management specialists/engineer technicians.

(6) When all user services are in agreement as to the action to be taken, the PICA will assume responsibility for procurement of kits, if required, for the total DOD program. Each SICA service is responsible for funding of kits equal to total installs plus retail stocks. The user services establish I&S relationships to include identification of I&S relationships in their respective ECPs.

(7) If universal agreement cannot be reached on approval of engineering changes, the PICA may elect to convene a Joint Service Configuration Control Board (JSCCB). The role of the PICA, as chairman of the JSCCB, is not to be construed as autonomous and abrogating individual service's peculiar requirements but rather to ensure that the requirements of all services are satisfied. If universal agreements cannot be reached, the PICA will insure that all costs of establishing a new item are fully portrayed and considered in the decision process, and the PICA/SICA relationships for both items will be negotiated with all user services. The new items resulting from an ECP must be reviewed by the original PICA for retention and will be retained for PICA management, except where justified otherwise by the PICA. This will help to reduce proliferation of item configurations and increase the standardization.

(8) The service opting for the new item will be responsible for the procurement of kits, funding of kits, and any additional supply pipeline stocks of the new item. If the PICA service is opting for the new item, the PICA shall negotiate with the nonconcurring SICAs for the nonreimbursable return of a quantity of old configuration wholesale stock, based upon a pro rata share of installed items. In no event will the PICA be required to provide more assets than were originally decapitalized by the SICA service.

(9) The same division of wholesale stocks may apply if the SICA is opting for the new configuration and the old configuration assets can be modified. The PICA assigned to the new item will be responsible for any kit procurement.

(10) The cost of incorporation of field level modifications accomplished below depot level will be funded by each service. The cost of incorporation of depot level modification of wholesale stocks will be funded by the PICA. Standard prices of reconfigured items will be adjusted as required. In the event a special depot retrofit program of SICA stocks is initiated, the PICA will arrange for such action with reimbursement by the SICA.

h. **Data Acquisition and Management:**

(1) The PICA will get required data applicable to multiused nonconsumables. SICAs will make sure SICA data requirements are submitted to and coordinated with the PICA.

(2) Technical Manuals. The PICA is responsible for the preparation, funding, acquisition, updating, and distribution of depot level maintenance technical manuals, the contents of which will be coordinated with the involved SICA. Each service will be responsible for preparation, funding, acquisition, updating, and distribution of service unique technical manuals. Where SICAs use the same contractual source for acquisition of technical manuals as the PICA, the SICA will acquire these services from the PICA.

(3) Engineering Drawings. The PICA will have sole responsibility for communicating with the design agency or contractor concerning engineering drawing revisions resulting from approved changes and the technical files of the PICA will be used to support the item. The policy and procedural guidance of DOD 4130.2M, on collaboration of changes to items of supply, will be used.

(4) Data Management. The PICA will coordinate the exchange of maintenance and operational data in line with the following:

(a) The DOD component which has design cognizance for an item is responsible for acquiring or developing and maintaining the technical data for the item, even if another DOD component has inventory management responsibility for that item.

(b) The technical files and data of the PICA will be used to support the item. If the PICA or the SICA considers its data to be deficient, supplemental or updated information and documentation will be identified, secured and recorded. The PICA and SICA will promptly interchange any design specification or drawing changes affecting the item.

(c) When technical data needs revision or clarification, the PICA will communicate with the appropriate design agency and the SICA, making known the need. The SICA will keep the PICA informed of the SICA service requirements.

(d) If the PICA no longer uses the nonconsumable item and a new PICA has been assigned for that item, the technical data package will be offered to the new PICA.

(e) In those instances where engineering inspection, analysis and/or testing of the failed or deficient item is required, the PICA service will provide complete instructions for marking and delivering of the item to the engineering site. The PICA service will fund engineering costs incurred from action initiated by the PICA. The SICA service will fund the cost incurred in action initiated by the SICA.

(f) Nonconsumable items that have special technical reporting requirements, (i.e., logbooks, depot maintenance data collection system, or reliability centered maintenance) concerning the operation and maintenance of the equipment will have the appropriate data entered in the applicable document. This will be done by all activities, (operating, maintenance, and overhaul) within the SICA and PICA services when such data are required by either the SICA or PICA. The SICA and PICA services will use their existing formats and procedures for this data recording.

i. **Quality Assurance (QA).** The PICA will be responsible for the QA requirements for multiused nonconsumables. The SICAs will provide requirements and support the QA program requirements. Particular emphasis will be placed on the following aspects of QA:

(1) The applicability of reliability and maintainability tests and demonstration results to in-process and completed end items.

(2) The QA support of first article tests and demonstration as well as production QA requirements.

(3) The quality deficiency report (QDR) will be in accordance with the requirements of DLAR 4155.24/AR 702-7/ NAVMATINST 4855.8B/AFR 74-6/MCO 4855.5B and individual service supplements. The PICA and SICA will conform to the deficiency reporting requirements of QDR priorities, forwarding across component lines, screening and action points and response time as specified in the joint regulation.

j. **Engineering Responsibility:**

(1) The PICA, in addition to providing engineering support for the PICA service, will coordinate all related joint service engineering actions.

(2) The SICA will coordinate any proposed engineering changes with the original equipment PICA.

(3) The PICA engineering/design activity will conduct first article tests and demonstrations.

(4) In those instances where the engineering responsibility has been assigned to a service different than the PICA in connection with a higher indenture (i.e., program, weapon, system equipment), the PICA will get required engineering support from that service.

(5) The PICA is responsible for engineering applicable to depot maintenance specification and coordinating such engineering with the SICA.

(6) The PICA is responsible for providing depot maintenance engineering support as requested by the SICA in support of SICA engineering needs. Such support will be on a reimbursable basis.

(7) Each service will define all aspects of the maintenance plan and provide the plan to the PICA.

k. **Depot Maintenance Specifications:**

(1) The PICA and SICA will negotiate a mutually agreeable standard maintenance specification. The PICA will initiate the specification and coordinate with the SICA. Contents of any changes will be agreed upon by negotiation and mutual consent before being incorporated into the standard specifications.

(2) When mutual consent cannot be obtained for revisions to joint specifications, the nonconcurring SICA activity will be reassigned to NIMSC 8. That activity will negotiate with the PICA for the return of an appropriate portion of the wholesale stock to reconstitute a SICA wholesale stock. In no event will the PICA be required to provide more assets than were originally furnished as wholesale assets by the nonconcurring service.

(3) When maintenance is performed by the PICA in a government-owned and government-operated facility, the PICA will maintain an adequate QA program using its established procedures.

(4) When maintenance is performed by the PICA by contract with commercial activities, the PICA (if it has QA cognizance) will make sure that the contractor maintains a quality system in accordance with the provisions of MIL-Q-9858A or MIL-I-45208A, as applicable, and delivers material of acceptable quality. If the PICA doesn't have QA cognizance of the contract, the DOD component which has QA cognizance, maintains a quality system according to MIL-Q-9858A or MIL-I-45208A, as applicable, and delivers material of acceptable quality. The SICA will deal with the PICA in all QA and contract management matters. If contractor won't bid with the restrictions of MIL-Q-9858A and MIL-I-45208A as a part of the contract then, as a minimum, the contractor must provide a Certificate of Conformance.

(5) For organic or contractual work, the PICA or the SICA can require a special examination of the quality system by a team of QA personnel. The necessity for the special examination will be determined by agreement between the PICA and the SICA. For organic work, the PICA will conduct the examination and invite SICA to participate. For contractual work, the cognizant contract administration office will conduct the examination, and invite other interested persons.

(6) Teardown deficiency reports (TDR) or disassembly inspection reports (DIR) may be requested at any time. Routine TDRs/DIRs are considered to be those which can be accomplished during the normal schedule of depot maintenance with little or no disruption. However, TDRs/DIRs other than routine, need separate funding.

(7) Provisions will be made for economic repair limitations in each depot maintenance specification.

Chapter 9

MATERIEL RETURNS (NIMSC 5 AND 6)

9-1. General. Uniform procedures for reporting and controlling the movement of nonconsumable items between the services will be incorporated into MILSTRIP. These procedures will address two conditions.

    a. Unserviceable assets being returned under credit/exchange arrangement.

    b. Serviceable excess assets.

9-2. Credit/Exchange Assets:

    a. Policy:

        (1) All unserviceable NIMSC 5 items (condition code E, F only) shall be returned to the designated PICA collection point. SICA-generated condemned items (condition H) won't be returned to the PICA, but will be disposed of in accordance with SICA instructions.

        (2) The PICA will provide credit (equal to 65 percent of the standard price) to the SICA for all returned NIMSC 5 unserviceable assets when a replacement requisition is being submitted. Such credit will be applied when the unserviceable asset is received by the PICA.

    b. Procedures:

        (1) All unserviceable NIMSC 5 items are subject to return to the designated PICA collection point. The PICA will provide the SICA with disposition instructions for all unserviceable NIMSC 5 items so the information can be incorporated into the SICA's materiel returns item listing. This listing will provide the PICA collection point shipping address transportation priority and other essential information.

        (2) The SICA will provide reimbursement to the PICA for assets issued. The PICA will provide credit to the SICA for all unserviceable assets received by the PICA when a replacement requisition has been submitted.

        (3) Credit will be granted by the PICA for SICA unserviceable returns after receipt and recording in the accountable records. The credit allowed will be shown in the next billing and collection cycle.

        (4) For items being repaired on commercial contract, the PICA will make sure the repair contract provides for the contractor to furnish the PICA with an image copy of the DD Form 1348-1 return document. This will be used by the PICA in granting proper credit to the SICA.

        (5) For items being repaired by a SICA service for the PICA via DMISA, the SICA must ensure that the repair activity provides copies of the DD Form 1348-1, DOD Single Line Item Release/Receipt Document, receiving document to the PICA for unserviceable NIMSC 5 items shipped from other than PICA activities. This will be used by the PICA in granting proper credit to the SICA.

        (6) SICA will generate FTA document (Notification of Return of Unserviceable Asset) for all unserviceable NIMSC 5 returns. The FTA will contain the appropriate project code when a replacement requisition for a serviceable item has been or will be submitted to the PICA.

        (7) The SICA generated turn-in document for unserviceable NIMSC 5 items (DD 1348-1) will also contain the appropriate project code when a replacement requisition for a serviceable item has been or will be submitted.

        (8) When a replacement requisition for an unserviceable NIMSC 5 item won't be submitted, the Project Code Field in the FTA and turn in document will be blank and credit won't be provided the SICA.

        (9) The PICA will follow up to SICA if an unserviceable asset has not been received within MILSTRIP materiel returns program time frames.

9-3. Excess Assets:

    a. Policy:

        (1) SICA service activities will report serviceable NIMSC 5 assets to their own service ICP according to SICA service criteria. SICAs will determine their service excess position and notify the PICA when assets are excess to established levels. Unserviceable excess NIMSC 5 items will be returned to the PICA in accordance with paragraph 9-2. SICA service activities for NIMSC 6 items will report excesses directly to the PICA.

        (2) The PICA will be the only DOD component authorized to approve disposal of reportable excess items.

        (3) The PICA will provide credit to the SICA for excess serviceable items when the PICA wholesale asset position is less than the consolidated AFAO.

    b. Procedures:

        (1) Reporting and responses between the SICA service and the PICA for excess serviceable items will be accomplished using FT-series documents in accordance with MILSTRIP.

      (2) Disposal of materiel at   PICA.
attrition sites will be as directed by the

OFFICIAL   CHARLES C. McDONALD, General, USAF
                                            Commander

FRANK A. MACHARONI, JR., Lt Col, USAF
Director of Information Management

THOMAS H. DOLAN   WILLIAM G. T. TUTTLE, JR.
Chief, Operations and Systems   General, USA
Integration Division   Commanding
                                            US Army Materiel Command

                                            C.A.H. TROST
                                            Admiral, United States Navy
                                            Chief of Naval Operations

          W.G. CARSON, JR., Lieutenant General, USMC
          Deputy Chief of Staff for Installations and Logistics
          Headquarters, U.S. Marine Corps

SUMMARY OF CHANGES
This revision includes revised JLC forms 17 and 19, and restructures the Defense
Integrated Materiel Management and Nonconsumable Item Program Committees to staff-to-staff
organizations rather than JLC subgroups. It also implements new policy changes relative
to interservice issues.

DISTRIBUTION SPECIAL

DEPARTMENT OF THE ARMY   2,626
   HQ AMC (AMCSM-MSM)
   5001 Eisenhower Ave, Alexandria, VA 22333-0001

   Letterkenny Army Depot
   ATTN: SDSLE-SAAD
   Chambersburg PA 17201   2,626

DEPARTMENT OF THE NAVY   500
   Defense Printing Service
   Room BD 831, Pentagon
   Washington, DC 20350   500

   (For DPS distribution 2 cys ea unless indicated)
   SNDL A5(MED only), C4K, FKA1 (10 cys ea), FKM13 (20 cys),
   FKM15 (20 cys), FKM17 (20 cys), FKN2 (Pt Hueneme only),
   FT64 Copy to: A3 (041), A4A (25 cys), 21A, FE1, FG1,
   FKA1F (20 cys), FT1, FKR73
   Stock: CO, NAVPUBFORMCEN, 5801 Tabor Ave, Phila PA 19120

DEPARTMENT OF THE AIR FORCE:
   F,X: 1,770
   PDO 4000A
   2750 ABW/IMPD
   Wright-Patterson AFB OH 45433   1,696
   Air Force Cryptological Support Center
   (MMLR), San Antonio TX 78243   35
   AFIT/LD   1
   AFCC (LGGS/LGML) Scott AFB IL 62225-5000 . . .   1
   HQ AFISC/IMP, Norton AFB CA 92409-7001   1
   AUL/LDEA, Maxwell AFB AL 36112-5564   1
   SSC/SMS, Gunter AFB AL 36114   3
   HQ USAF/LEY   5
   AFTEC/LG, Kirtland AFB NM 87117   1
   HQ ATC/IMPDD, Randolph AFB, TX 78150-5001 . .   1
   National Security Agency/S-53
   9800 Savage Rd, Ft George G.Meade MD 20755 . .   25

Marine Corps: 435
   CMC (Code HQSP-2)
   ARLEX, Room 1302
   Washington, DC 20380-0001   55

   Commanding General
   Marine Corps Logistics Base
   M/F: Pubs Stock, Warehouse 1221, Section 5
   Albany Georgia 31704-5001   380

National Weather Service (W/OSO322)   5
   8060 13th St
   Gramax Bldg, Rm 326
   Silver Spring, MD 20910

APPENDIX A

CERTIFICATE OF USABILITY

NATIONAL STOCK NUMBER	PRIMARY INVENTORY CONTROL ACTIVITY (PICA) CONTROL NO

SERVICE

PICA (Circle applicable code)				SICA (Circle applicable code for concurring SICA Service(s))			
A	N	F	M	A	N	F	M

The procurement specification and depot repair specification have been reviewed and are concurred with. The acceptance of these specifications is evidence that PICA/SICA wholesale stocks meeting the specifications may be issued to any activity of the signing PICA/SICA(s) service to satisfy the service requirement.

SERVICE	INVENTORY CONTROL POINT	CONCURRING/ORIGINATING OFFICIAL	DATE
ARMY			
NAVY			
AIR FORCE			
MARINE CORPS			

NONCONSUMABLE ITEM MATERIAL SUPPORT CODE

PICA	SICA (5 or 6 only)
EFFECTIVE TRANSFER DATE[2]	

REMARKS

[1] Enter the two-digit managing activity code which identifies the service activity responsible for primary/secondary item control
[2] Enter effective transfer date from checklist if SICA agrees. If SICA is not in agreement, enter SICA proposed effective transfer date

JLC FORM 16 JUN 80

APPENDIX B

ASSET REPORTING		REPORT CONTROL SYMBOL
INSTRUCTIONS		

This form is to be submitted 90 days prior to the Effective Transfer Date (ETD) for all indicated MILSTRAP condition codes. Both the current quantity of assets (as of submission date) and the quantity projected to be available on ETD will be reported. On ETD, the asset report will be resubmitted for MILSTRAP condition codes G, J, K, L, and M. The second column indicating "QUANTITY" on "ETD" will be the only column completed. The SICA will cite the Report Control Symbol (RCS) of the PICA when completing this report. The following report control symbols apply:

AF:	RCS: LOG-MM(AR)7807	NAVY:	RCS: NAVSUP 4790-2
ARMY:	RCS: ORCMM-325	MARINE CORPS:	RCS: SP-4410-14

NATIONAL STOCK NUMBER	SUBMITTING SERVICE ICP	DATE OF SUBMISSION
CONDITION CODE	**CURRENT QUANTITY**	**PROJECT QNTY · QNTY ON ETD**
A (SERVICEABLE - ISSUABLE WITHOUT QUALIFICATIONS)		
B (SERVICEABLE - ISSUABLE WITH QUALIFICATIONS)		
C (SERVICEABLE - PRIORITY ISSUE)		
D (SERVICEABLE - TEST / MODIFICATION)		
E (UNSERVICEABLE - LIMITED RESTORATION)		
F (UNSERVICEABLE - REPARABLE)		
G (UNSERVICEABLE - INCOMPLETE)		
J (SUSPENDED - IN STOCK)		
K (SUSPENDED - RETURNS)		
L (SUSPENDED - LITIGATION)		
M (SUSPENDED - IN WORK)		
DUE IN FROM CONTRACT		
DELIVERY SCHEDULE		
PROCUREMENT IN PROCESS		
DUE IN FROM RECLAMATION		
DUE IN FROM FIELD ACTIVITIES		
REMARKS		

SAMPLE

JLC FORM 15, JAN 89   PREVIOUS EDITION IS OBSOLETE

40

APPENDIX C

INSTRUCTIONS FOR COMPLETING
REQUIREMENTS DATA EXCHANGE CARD

The Requirements Data Exchange Card (RDEC) will be used by the SICAs to pass projected requirements data to the PICA. SICA prepositioned war reserve (PWR) requirements, initial provisioning/outfitting (Initial Spares Support List) requirements and follow-on provisioning/outfitting (Follow-on Spares Support List) requirements will not normally be included on RDECs, since these requirements will not normally be requisitioned from PICA wholesale stocks. The procurement lead time for these requirements will be budgeted by the SICA. These items will normally be procured using MIPR, submitted procurement lead time prior to need. Five years of data (projected requisitioning requirements and projected unserviceable returns) will be completed and submitted annually to arrive at the PICA by 1 February with an effective date of 31 March for each SICA NIMSC 5 item (zeros must also be submitted.) Projected data may be resubmitted during the year as required with an effective date of the last day of fiscal year quarter. Projected data should be reviewed during the annual September stratification process for resubmission. SICA NIMSC 6 items require a one-time submission of the RDEC 90 days before the effective date of the NIMSC 6. RDEC submission will be by batch processing through automatic digital network (AUTODIN). Content Indicator Code IHAE applies. Positions 1-25, header data, will be duplicated on all transactions forwarded to the PICA. All quantitative data fields will be zero filled to the left.

Transaction 1

Positions	Instructions
1-3	Enter document identifier WR1.
4-6	Enter the routing identifier of the PICA activity to which the data transactions are being forwarded.
7	Blank.
8-22	Enter the national stock number.
23-25	Enter the routing identifier of the SICA activity forwarding the RDEC.
26-29	Enter the last digit of the calendar year and Julian date requirements are submitted.
30	Enter the SICA NIMSC.
31-36	Blank.
37-42	Enter the OWRMR.
43-48	Blank.
49-50	Enter the last two digits of the current fiscal year.
51-70	Recurring Demand Projected Requirements Current fiscal year.
51-55	1st Qtr(Zero fill)
55-60	2d Qtr(Zero fill)
61-65	3d Qtr(Zero fill)
66-70	4th Qtr(Zero fill)
71-78	Blank
79-80	Enter a 1 in position 79. Position 80 will be blank.

Transaction 2

Position	Instructions
1-25	Duplicate entries in positions 1-25 of transaction 1
26-45	Recurring demand Projected Requirements-Current year plus one.
26-30	1st Qtr(Zero fill)
31-35	2d Qtr(Zero fill)
36-40	3d Qtr(Zero fill)

Positions	Instructions
41-45	4th Qtr(Zero fill)
46-65	Recurring demand Projected Requirements-Current fiscal year plus two.
46-50	1st Qtr(Zero fill)
51-55	2d Qtr(Zero fill)
56-60	3d Qtr(Zero fill)
61-65	4th Qtr(Zero fill)
65-75	Recurring demand Projected Requirements-Current fiscal year plus three.
66-70	1st Qtr(Zero fill)
71-75	2d Qtr(Zero fill)
76-78	Perpetuate data from transaction 1 positions 27-29.
79-80	Enter a 2 in position 79. Position 80 will be blank.

Transaction 3

Positions	Instructions
1-25	Duplicate entries in positions 1-25 of transaction 1.
26-35	Recurring demand Projected Requirements-Current fiscal year plus three (continued).
26-30	3d Qtr(Zero fill)
31-35	4th Qtr(Zero fill)
36-55	Recurring demand Projected Requirements-Current fiscal year plus four.
36-40	1st Qtr(Zero fill)
41-45	2d Qtr(Zero fill)
46-50	1st Qtr(Zero fill)
51-55	4th Qtr(Zero fill)
56-75	Projected Unserviceable Returns-Current fiscal year.
56-60	1st Qtr(Zero fill)
61-65	2d Qtr(Zero fill)
66-70	3d Qtr(Zero fill)
71-75	4th Qtr(Zero fill)
76-78	Perpetuate data from transaction 1 positions 27-29.
79-80	Enter a 3 in position 79. Position 80 will be blank.

Transaction 4

Positions	Instructions
1-25	Duplicate entries in positions 1-25 of transaction 1.
26-45	Projected Unserviceable Returns Current fiscal year plus one.
26-30	1st Qtr(Zero fill)
31-35	2d Qtr(Zero fill)
36-40	3d Qtr(Zero fill)
41-45	4th Qtr(Zero fill)
46-65	Projected Unserviceable Returns Current-fiscal year plus two.
46-50	1st Qtr(Zero fill)
51-55	2d Qtr(Zero fill)
56-60	3d Qtr(Zero fill)
61-65	4th Qtr(Zero fill)
66-75	Projected Unserviceable Returns-Current fiscal year plus three.
66-70	1st Qtr(Zero fill)
71-75	2d Qtr(Zero fill)
76-78	Perpetuate data from transaction 1 positions 27-29.
79-80	Enter a 4 in position 79. Position 80 will be blank.

Transaction 5

Positions	Instructions
1-25	Duplicate entries in positions 1-25 of transaction 1.
26-35	Projected Unserviceable Returns - Current fiscal year plus three (continued).
26-30	3d Qtr (Zero fill)
31-35	4th Qtr (Zero fill)
36-55	Projected Unserviceable Returns - Current fiscal year plus four.
36-40	1st Qtr (Zero fill)
41-45	2d Qtr (Zero fill)
46-50	3d Qtr (Zero fill)
51-55	4th Qtr (Zero fill)
56-75	Projected Nonrecurring Requirements - Current fiscal year. (Exclude PWRS, initial provisioning/outfitting (ISSL), follow-on provisioning/outfitting (FOSSL) requirements, procurement lead time requirements budgeted by SICA and to be funded by SICA MIPR-a procurement lead time in advance of SICA MSD.)
56-60	1st Qtr (Zero fill)
61-65	2d Qtr (Zero fill)
66-70	3d Qtr (Zero fill)
71-75	4th Qtr (Zero fill)
76-78	Perpetuate data from transaction 1 positions 27-29.
79	Enter a "5".
80	If nonrecurring requirements are projected, position 80 will be blank. If no nonrecurring requirements are projected, enter an E to indicate last transaction for item. If E is entered in position 80, transactions 6 and 7 will not be submitted.

Transaction 6

Positions	Instructions
1-25	Duplicate entries in positions 1-25 of transaction 1.
26-45	Projected Nonrecurring Requirements - Current fiscal year plus one. (Exclude PWRS, initial provisioning/outfitting (ISSL), follow-on provisioning-outfitting (FOSSL) requirements, procurement lead-time requirements, and other requirements budgeted by SICA and to be funded by SICA MIPR a procurement lead time in advance of SICA MSD).
26-30	1st Qtr (Zero fill)
31-35	2d Qtr (Zero fill)
36-40	3d Qtr (Zero fill)
41-45	4th Qtr (Zero fill)
46-65	Projected Nonrecurring Requirements - Current fiscal year plus two. (Exclude PWRS, initial provisioning/outfitting (ISSL), follow-on provisioning/outfitting (FOSSL) requirements, procurement lead-time requirements, and other requirements budgeted by SICA and to be funded by SICA MIPR a procurement lead time in advance of SICA MSD).
46-50	1st Qtr (Zero fill)
51-55	2d Qtr (Zero fill)
56-60	3d Qtr (Zero fill)
61-65	4th Qtr (Zero fill)
66-75	Projected Nonrecurring Requirements - Current fiscal year plus three. (Exclude PWRS, initial provisioning/ outfitting (ISSL), follow-on provisioning/outfitting (FOSSL) requirements, procurement lead-time requirements, and other requirements budgeted by SICA and to be funded by SICA MIPR a procurement lead time in advance of SICA MSD).
66-70	1st Qtr (Zero fill)
71-75	2d Qtr (Zero fill)
76-78	Perpetuate data from transaction 1 positions 27-29. 79-80 Enter a 6 in position 79. Position 80 will be blank.

Transaction 7

Positions   *Instructions*

1-25   Duplicate entries in positions 1-25 of   transaction 1.

26-35   Projected Nonrecurring Requirements - Current fiscal   year plus three
            (continued). (Exclude PWRS, initial provisioning/outfitting (ISSL),
            follow-on provisioning/outfitting (FOSSL) requirements,   procurement
            lead-time requirements, and other requirements budgeted by SICA and
            to be funded by SICA MIPR a procurement lead-time in advance of SICA
            MSD)

26-30   3d Qtr (Zero fill)

31-35   4th Qtr (Zero fill)

36-55   Projected Nonrecurring Requirements - Current fiscal   year plus four.
            (Exclude PWRS, initial provisioning/outfitting (ISSL), follow-on
            provisioning/outfitting (FOSSL) requirements, procurement lead-time
            requirements, and other requirements budgeted by SICA and to be
            funded by SICA MIPR a procurement lead time in advance of SICA
            MSD.)

36-40   1st Qtr (Zero fill)

41-45   2d Qtr (Zero fill)

46-50   3d Qtr (Zero fill)

51-55   4th Qtr (Zero fill)

56-78   Blank.

79   Enter a 7.

80   Enter an E to indicate last transaction for item.

44

APPENDIX D

NONCONSUMABLE ITEM MATERIEL SUPPORT REQUEST
JLC FORM 17

1. The NIMSR has been established to obtain initial support and recordation of the SICA in the DLSC TIR. Forms may be locally reproduced as required. Once the SICA is recorded as a user, the NIMSR won't be used to obtain follow on support.

2. Instructions for completing the NIMSR are as follows: The form will be submitted in duplicate to the PICA. The requesting service will complete Part I. Upon receipt, the PICA will complete Part II and return the NIMSR to the SICA within 45 days. The PICA/ SICAs will be responsible for identifying the cognizant configuration manager in its involved service in Part I, block 13 and Part II, block 12. One copy of the completed NIMSR will be returned to the SICA; NIMSR Focal Point and one copy will be retained by the PICA for its records. Information copies will be provided by the PICA to all configuration organizations identified. Additional information may be provided in the remarks block on the back of the form.

PART I

The requesting activity will complete the NIMSR as follows:

FROM: Enter your one position service code (A=Army, B=FAA, C=Coast Guard, F=Air Force, M=Marine Corps, N=Navy) and the two-position alpha managing activity code, contact name, address (including office symbol/code), and automatic voice network (AUTOVON) phone number.

TO: Enter the one position service code, two-position alpha managing activity code, and the mailing address of the PICA managing activity.

BLOCK 1: Enter the NSN. If the NSN desired is in a DOD I&S family relationship, the master NSN must be entered here.

BLOCK 1A: If AF managed, enter MMAC code, if applicable. If Navy managed, enter COG code, if applicable. Otherwise, leave blank.

BLOCK 2: Enter the primary part number.

BLOCK 3: Enter the type of weapon system/end item application.

BLOCK 3A: Enter the number of weapon system/end items being supported.

BLOCK 4: Enter requested SICA NIMSC to indicate the level of support the PICA is being requested to provide.

BLOCK 4A: Check appropriate block to advise the PICA if a TRP will be required for Phase II review.

BLOCK 5: Enter the item(s) repairability code.

BLOCK 5A: Enter the MLC to indicate management technique to be applied. (E = Depot Reparable Component, D = End Item of Equipment, R = Consumable, U = Special Management)

BLOCK 6: Enter the appropriate MOE rule to be established in the DLSC TIR.

BLOCK 7: Enter the number of installs that will be required.

BLOCK 8: Enter one of the following codes to indicate the type of program used to determine item requirement: (H = Hours, M = Miles, R = Rounds, S = Starts, L = Landings, D = Days, T = months, Y = Years).

BLOCK 9: If the desired NSN is in a DODI + S family relationship, list all related NSNS that you want to become a user on. Use block 15 or the back of the form if more space is required.

BLOCK 10: Enter the projected annual operational usage, e.g., 150,000 hours, 800 months, 600 overhauls, etc.

BLOCK 10A: Enter the initial quantity required.

BLOCK 10B: Enter the date the initial quantity is required.

BLOCK 10C: Enter the date support is desired for Phase II (NIMSC 5, 6) only. Applicable only if TRP is not required.

BLOCK 11: Entry required only if block 4 is NIMSC 5 or 6. Enter projected replenishment demand by year for 5 years. (A through E are years 1-5).

BLOCK 12: Entry required only if block 4 is NIMSC 5 or 6. Enter the projected unserviceable assets to be returned to the PICA for the corresponding 5 year period identified in block 11. (A through E are years 1-5.)

BLOCK 13: Enter the mailing address of the cognizant configuration/engineering management organization element in the SICA service.

BLOCK 14: Enter the SICA internal suspense control number.

BLOCK 15: Enter additional data if necessary.

BLOCK 16: Enter the signature and title of the requesting official and the date signed.

PART II

The PICA will enter information in the Part II blocks of the NIMSR (JLC Form 17) as follows:

FROM: Enter your one-position service code, two-position alpha managing activity code, contact name, address (including office symbol/code), and AUTOVON phone number.

TO: Enter the one-position service code, two-position alpha managing activity code, and the address.

BLOCK 1: Check appropriate box to concur or nonconcur with the NIMSC requested in Part I, block 4.

BLOCK 2: If nonconcurrence in block 1, provide justification and PICA proposed NIMSC.

BLOCK 3: Enter the method (MIPR or funded requisition) by which the initial quantity will be supported.

BLOCK 4: Enter the number of months which will elapse between receipt of a SICA MIPR/ requisition and the time materiel will be available for release to the SICA.

BLOCK 5: Enter the date the MIPR or funded requisition is required by the PICA. (Materiel support date (Part II, block 8) minus procurement lead-time (Part II, block 4) minus PICA administrative MIPR processing time.)

BLOCK 6: Enter the item(s) unit cost(s).

BLOCK 7: Enter the total dollar value to be cited when materiel is to be provided via MIPR.

BLOCK 8: When NIMSC requested is 5 or 6 (Part I, block 4) and the PICA concurs (Part II Block 1), enter the date when support can be provided.

BLOCK 9: For NIMSC 5 items, enter the DODAAD code and address for the activity where unserviceables are to be shipped.

BLOCK 10: Enter the PICA document control number.

BLOCK 11: Enter the date the catalog data was submitted to DLSC.

BLOCK 12: Enter the mailing address of the cognizant configuration/engineering management organization element in the SICA service.

BLOCK 13: Enter additional data (or overflow from other blocks) as required.

BLOCK 14: Enter the signature and title of the approving official and the date signed.

APPENDIX D

NONCONSUMABLE ITEM MATERIEL SUPPORT REQUEST

PART I	SICA REQUESTING ORGANIZATION

FROM (SVC Code, Mgt Code, Name, Address, Phone)   TO (SVC Code, Mgt Code, Address)

1 NSN (Master)	1A. AF MMAC, NAVY COG CODE	2 PRIMARY PART NUMBER		
3. WEAPON SYSTEM - END ITEM APPLICATION	3A. NUMBER OF SYSTEMS SUPPORTED	4. LEVEL OF SUPPORT (NIMSC)	4A. TECHNICAL REVIEW PACKAGE (TRP) REQUIRED ☐ YES ☐ NO	5 REPAIRABILITY CODE	5A MGT LEVEL CODE (MLC)
6. MAJOR ORGANIZATIONAL ENTITY (MOE) RULE	7. INSTALLED QTY.	8. TYPE PROGRAM	9 NSN (Suitable Subs)		
10 OPERATIONAL ANNUAL USAGE	10A. INITIAL QUANTITY	10B. DATE INITIAL QUANTITY REQUIRED	10C. REQUESTED MATERIAL SUPPORT DATE		

11 REPLENISHMENT DEMAND   12 UNSERVICEABLE RETURNS

A	B	C	D	E	A	B	C	D	E

13 SICA CONFIGURATION MANAGER	14 SICA CONTROL NUMBER	15. REMARKS

16 SIGNATURE AND TITLE OF REQUESTING OFFICIAL	DATE

PART II	PICA RESPONSE

FROM (SVC Code, Mgt Code, Name, Address, Phone)   TO (SVC Code, Mgt Code, Address)

1 LEVEL OF SUPPORT (NIMSC) ☐ CONCUR ☐ NONCONCUR	2 JUSTIFICATION	
3 METHOD OF SUPPORT FOR INITIAL QUANTITY	4 PROCUREMENT LEAD TIME (Months)	5 DATE FUNDS REQUIRED
6 UNIT COST	7 TOTAL DOLLAR VALUE	8 APPROVED MATERIAL SUPPORT DATE	9 UNSERVICEABLE RECEIVING ACTIVITY (DODAAD Address)
10 DOCUMENT CONTROL NUMBER	11 DATE SUBMITTED TO DLSC	12 PICA CONFIGURATION MANAGER

13 REMARKS

14 SIGNATURE AND TITLE OF APPROVING OFFICIAL	DATE

JLC FORM 17, MAY 87   PREVIOUS EDITION IS OBSOLETE

APPENDIX E

INSTRUCTIONS FOR CONTENTS CHECKLIST
JLC FORM 18

A review package will be assembled by the PICA for each item eligible for PHASE II consideration. This package will be provided to each SICA for review and will include a checklist to identify the contents. SICAs will accomplish necessary reviews to determine acceptability of procurement, repair, and packaging specifications and return the package with a signed copy of the Certificate of Usability when specifications are concurred with. In those instances where concurrence is not obtained, reasons for nonconcurrence and/or the revisions required to PICA specifications which, if incorporated, would result in SICA concurrence will be returned to the PICA. The SICA review is to be completed and the package returned to the PICA within 120 days from the date of the PICA transmittal letter.

1. Enter the service and managing activity code of the PICA.

2. Enter the item name.

3. Enter the NSN.

4. Enter the applicable PICA management level code as follows:
     D Major End Item
     E Reparable Item
     R Consumable Item
     U Special Management

5. Enter the CAGE and manufacturer's part number (PN).

6. List procurement data enclosed with package.

7. Enter the Procurement Method Code (PMC).

8. Enter the SMR Code.

9. List repair data enclosed with package. If repair specifications are included in a technical order which is known to be available to the SICA ICP, identify the technical order and applicable section instead of forwarding the document itself.

10. List proposed credit for unserviceable returns.

11. Enter the control number of the DMISA in force.

12. The proposed ETD will normally be set at 270 days from the date of the letter which transmits the item data package for review.

13. Enter the Department of Defense Activity Address Directory (DODAAD) code of the PICA collection point designated to receive assets subject to automatic returns.

14. Enter the application of the item.

15. Enter the packaging specifications.

16. Enter remarks, if required.

CONTENTS CHECKLIST	
1. SUBMITTING ACTIVITY	2. ITEM NAME
3. NATIONAL STOCK NUMBER	4. MANAGEMENT LEVEL CODE
5. FSCM AND MANUFACTURER'S PART NUMBER	6. PROCUREMENT DATA ENCLOSED
7. PROCUREMENT METHOD CODE	8. SOURCE MAINTENANCE AND RECOVERABILITY CODE 9. REPAIR DATA ENCLOSED
10. PROPOSED CREDIT FOR UNSERVICEABLE RETURNS	11. DMISA ☐ YES ☐ NO DMISA CONTROL NO.
12. PROPOSED EFFECTIVE TRANSFER DATE	13. RECEIVING ACTIVITY FOR REPARABLES
14. APPLICATION	15. PACKAGING SPECIFICATION
16. REMARKS	

JLC FORM 18 JUN 81   REPLACES AFLC FORM 166, MAR 76, WHICH WILL BE USED

50

APPENDIX F

INSTRUCTIONS FOR PREPARING, PICA/SICA MANAGEMENT LEVEL CHANGE AND/OR REASSIGNMENT REQUEST JLC FORM 19

1. Request has been established for use when recommending transfer of PICA and when changing level of item management. Reproduction of this form is the responsibility of each requiring service.

2. Instructions for completing the JLC Form 19 are as follows. The requesting office will complete Part I (blocks 1-14) and mail to the involved service ICP. The receiving ICP will complete Part II (blocks 1-6).

PART I

To be completed by the requesting activity as follows:

FROM: Enter your one position service code (A=Army, F=Air Force, M=Marine Corps, N=Navy, B=FAA, C=Coast Guard), two position alpha managing activity code, contact name, address (including office symbol/code), and AUTOVON phone number.

TO: Enter the one position service code, two position alpha managing activity code, and the address.

BLOCK 1: Enter the NSN. If the NSN desired is in a DOD I&S family relationship, the master NSN must be entered here.

BLOCK 2: Enter the primary part number.

BLOCK 3: Enter the type of weapon system/end item being supported.

BLOCK 4: Enter the noun (item name).

BLOCK 5: If the desired NSN is in a DOD I&S family relationship, list all NSNs in the family (continue on back).

BLOCK 6: Enter the item unit price.

BLOCK 7A: Enter the two position alpha managing activity codes to identify the changes being proposed.

BLOCK 7B: Enter the proposed management level change.

BLOCK 8: Check the appropriate box. Attach any necessary rationale for requesting the change.

BLOCK 9: Enter demand and stockage data and current item management code.

BLOCK 10: Enter the current and proposed data elements requiring change. If "Service Use Discontinued" is checked in Block 7, note any continuing Foreign Military Sales (FMS) support requirements by inserting the applicable "FMS Sponsor Only" MOE Rule in the "SICA TO" space.

BLOCK 11: Enter the name, office symbol/code, and AUTOVON phone number of the individual to be contacted regarding this form.

BLOCK 12: Enter the response due date. Allow time based on the on the following standards:
    60 days - NIMSC changes within Phase I, deletion of SICA MOE rule, other.
    90 days - SICA request for NIMSC changes from Phase I to Phase II or vice versa

120 days - Deletion of PICA Moe rule of PICA Reassignment
180 days - MLC Change, PICA request for NIMSC change from Phase I to Phase II

BLOCK 13: Do not fill in for consumables. Must be filled in for changes from consumables to nonconsumables.

BLOCK 13A: Enter the specification/publication number.

BLOCK 13B: Enter estimated repair costs.

BLOCK 13C: Enter 65% for NIMSC 5 items.

BLOCK 13D: Enter activity code of repair facility.

BLOCK 14: Enter name, title, and signature of requesting official.

PART II

To be completed by the approving activity and returned to the requesting activity as follows:

FROM: Enter your one position service code, two position alpha managing activity code, contact name, address (including office symbol/code), and AUTOVON phone number.

TO: Enter the one position service code, two position alpha managing activity code, and the address.

BLOCK 1: Mark either "concur" or "nonconcur." Explain nonconcurrence in "Remarks" block on back of form.

BLOCK 2: Enter approved NIMSC. If losing manager, also enter MOE Rule.

BLOCK 3: Enter your document control number.

BLOCK 4: Enter the ETD.

BLOCK 5: Enter the MSD.

BLOCK 6: Enter the name, title and signature of the approving official and the date signed.

APPENDIX F

PICA / SICA MANAGEMENT LEVEL CHANGE AND / OR REASSIGNMENT REQUEST	DATE

PART I — TO BE COMPLETED BY THE REQUESTING OFFICE

FROM (SVC Code, Mgt Code, Name, Address, Phone) | TO (SVC Code, Mgt Code, Address)

1 NATIONAL STOCK NUMBER (Master)	2. PRIMARY PART NUMBER	3. APPLICATION
4. ITEM NAME	5. NSN (Suitable Sub)	6. UNIT PRICE

7 ACTION (s) RECOMMENDED BY THE PICA / SICA FOR CONCURRENCE

A. REASSIGNMENT OF PICA / SICA RESPONSIBILITY FROM MANAGING ACTIVITY CODE _____ TO _____

B. CHANGE IN MANAGEMENT LEVEL CODE FROM (Check Applicable Box) TO
☐ CONSUMABLE ☐ NONCONSUMABLE
☐ CONSUMABLE ☐ NONCONSUMABLE

8 REASON FOR REQUEST (Attach Rationale)

☐ ECONOMIC OR TECHNICAL FACTORS
☐ DEPOT MAINTENANCE ASSIGNMENT
☐ OTHER (Explain)
☐ SERVICE USE DISCONTINUED
☐ COLLOCATION OF MANAGEMENT
☐ LOGISTICS REASSIGNMENTS

9. OTHER INFORMATION

LAST 2 YEARS DEMAND	QUANTITY ON HAND	DUE IN QUANTITY	DUE OUT QUANTITY	ITEM MANAGEMENT CODE

10 DATA TO BE CHANGED ARE

DATA ELEMENTS AFFECTED	PICA		SICA	
	FROM	TO	FROM	TO
MOE RULE				
NIMSC				
CMD (AAC, Repair Code, etc)				
SM&R CODE				

11. POINT OF CONTACT	OFFICE SYMBOL CODE	PHONE	12. RESPONSE DUE DATE

13. REPAIR OVERHAUL SPECIFICATION PUBLICATION (If applicable) (Mandatory if changing from consumable to nonconsumable)

A. SPEC PUB NUMBER	B. EST OVERHAUL COST	C EST CREDIT FOR UNSVC RETURNS	D. OVERHAUL ACTIVITY CODE

14. TYPED NAME AND TITLE OF REQUESTING OFFICIAL	SIGNATURE OF REQUESTING OFFICIAL

PART II — TO BE COMPLETED BY THE APPROVING AUTHORITY

FROM (SVC Code, Mgt Code, Name, Address, Phone) | TO (SVC Code, Mgt Code, Address)

1. ☐ CONCUR _____ ☐ NONCONCUR _____

2. APPROVED NIMSC MOE RULE	3. DOCUMENT CONTROL NUMBER	4. PROPOSED EFFECTIVE TRANSFER DATE	5. MATERIEL SPT DATE

6 TYPED NAME AND TITLE OF APPROVING OFFICIAL	SIGNATURE OF APPROVING OFFICIAL	DATE

JLC FORM 19, MAY 87   PREVIOUS EDITION IS OBSOLETE

APPENDIX G

Interrogation Results of Other Service Inventory Control Points (ICPs)

1. **Formats:**

   a. **Interrogation.** Interrogation originated by the PICA will be prepared in accordance with the following format:

Field Legend	Positions	Explanation
Document Identifier	1-3	See paragraph 2C below.
Routing Identifier (To)	4-6	ICP being interrogated.
	7	Reserved.
National Stock Number	8-20	NSN of item required.
Service Management Codes	21-22	Management Aggregation of requiring ICP.
Unit of Issue	23-24	Two letter abbreviation.
Quantity	25-29	Quantity of time required.
Document Number	30-43	(1) 30-35 DOD Activity
Address code		(2) 36-39 Julian Date.
		(3) 40 J constant to denote interservice transaction.
		(4) 41-42 Control (serial) number.
Manufacturer's Code	44-48	Manufacturer's five-digit code.
Part Number	49-66	Part Number of required Item.
Routing Identifier (From)	67-69	Activity to which the reply should be sent.
	70-71	Reserved. Reimbursable/ Nonreimbursable
	72	Enter "1" if reimbursable Enter "2" if nonreimbursable
	73	Reserved.
Part Number	74-80	Continuation of long part number.

   b. **Reply.** Reply will be prepared by the SICA and submitted in accordance with the following format:

Field Legend	Positions	Explanation
Document Identifier	1-3	JSX.
Routing Identifier (To)	4-6	Originating Activity.
	7	Reserved.
National Stock Number	8-20	NSN of item offered.
Service Management Codes	21-22	Duplicated from the Interrogation transaction.
Unit of Issue	23-24	Two-letter abbreviation
Quantity	25-29	Quantity available.
Document Number	30-43	Duplicated from the interrogation.
Manufacturer	44-48	Manufacturer's five-digit code.
Part Number	49-66	P/N of offered item.
Routing Identifier (From)	67-69	Routing Identifier of Offering ICP.
I&S Code	70	Identifies potential interchangeable or substitute item being offered in lieu of item requested.
	71	Reserved. Reimbursable/ Nonreimbursable Code
	72	Enter "1" if reimbursable, and "2" if nonreimbursable.
Condition Code	73	Enter MILSTRAP condition code.
Unit Price	74-80	Standard unit price of offered item.

2. **Interrogation Message Formats.**
    a. **Message will contain the following data:**

    (1) Type Action.
    (2) Document Identifier.
    (3) Stock Number.
    (4) Unit of Issue.
    (5) Quantity Required.
    (6) Part Number.
    (7) Document Number.
    (8) Unit Price.

    b. **Replies to message interrogations will contain the following data:**

    (1) Type of Action.
    (2) Document Identifier.
    (3) Stock Number.
    (4) Unit of Issue.
    (5) Quantity Available.
    (6) MILSTRAP Condition Code.
    (7) Where Available.
    (8) Document Number.
    (9) Unit Price, if reimbursable.

    c. **Document Identifiers.**

    (1) Interrogation.

Code	Explanation
JTX	Used to interrogate other program participants for requirements. Issue Priority Group II (Priorities 04-08).
JTV	Used to interrogate other program participants for
JTZ	Used to interrogate other program participants for emergency requirements, Issue Priority Group I (Priorities 01-03).

    (2) Interrogation Reply.

Code	Explanation
JSX	Use to identify a reply to an interrogation.

APPENDIX H

TERMS

Approved Force Acquisition Objective- See DOD Directive 4100.37.

Authorized to be in Use- That quantity of end items of equipment authorized in accordance with individual service allowance documents.

Consumable Item- An item that is normally expended or used up beyond recovery in the use for which it was designed or intended.

Contract Maintenance- Any depot level maintenance performed under contract by commercial organizations, including original manufacturers.

Depot Maintenance Interservice Support Agreement (DMISA) - An agreement whereby one service (the agent) accomplishes depot level maintenance work for another service (the principal).

Depot Reparable Component- An item of durable nature which, when unserviceable, normally can be economically restored to a serviceable condition through regular repair procedures. An item which, when beyond the repair capability of lower level (organization/ intermediate) maintenance, is returned to the depot which possesses more extensive repair facilities. Condemnation and disposal is normally not authorized below depot level. Requirement determination by ICP considers projected unserviceable returns from using activities. When attached to or installed in another item, it losses its identity and becomes an integral part of the item in which it is attached or installed; for example, valves, fuel controls, truck transmissions, amplifiers, turbine wheels, actuators, etc.

Depot Source of Repair (DSOR)- A two-digit code assigned to each activity that performs depot maintenance on nonconsumable items. This code, which indicates the approved DSOR for each using service, is to be included for each nonconsumable item that is cataloged in the DIDS TIR. The MISMO is the only approval authority for establishing DIDS DSOR data for that service.

End Item- An NSN item which is a final combination of end products, component parts, and material which is ready for its intended use and retains its identity during use. Requirements are normally based on authorization documents, such as tables of basic allowances or tables of organization and equipment. Asset visibility is not normally maintained by the ICP when the item is in the hands of the user; for example, vehicles, ground starting units, generator sets, electronic test equipment, oscilloscopes, etc.

Inconsistent Item- An item which the using military services manage differently from each other, i.e. in some combination of end items, depot reparable components, consumables and/ or special management items.

Inventory Control Point (ICP)- An organizational unit or activity within a DOD supply system which is assigned the primary responsibility for the materiel management of a group of items either for a particular service or for the Defense Department as a whole. Materiel management normally includes cataloging direction, requirements computation, procurement direction, distribution management, disposal direction and generally, rebuild direction, or agency designated to exercise Integrated Materiel Management for an FSC group/class, commodity, or item on a DOD or Federal Government-wide basis.

Interchangeability and Substitutability (I&S):
    a. **Interchangeable Item**- An item which, (1) possesses such functional and physical characteristics as to be equivalent in performance, reliability, and maintainability to another item of similar or identical purpose; and (2) is capable of being exchanged for the other item without alteration of the items themselves or of adjoining items, except for adjustment.

   b. Substitute Item- An item which possesses such functional and physical characteristics as to be capable of being exchanged for another only under specified conditions or for particular applications and without alteration of the items themselves or of adjoining items. This term is synonymous with the phrase, "One way interchangeability," such as item B can be interchanged in all applications for item A, but item A cannot be used in all applications requiring Item B.

Joint Policy Coordinating Group on Defense Integrated Materiel Management (JPCG/DIMM)- A policy coordinating group established by the Joint Logistics Commanders to serve as a communication link among the military logistics commands to further progress toward the objective of integrated management.

Joint Policy Coordinating Group for Depot Maintenance Interservicing (JPCG-DMI)- A policy coordinating group chartered by the Joint Logistics Commanders to establish specific maintenance interservice policy and provide for a definitive action program on a continuing basis.

Level of Authority (LOA) Rule- A code that identifies the LOA of a PICA or a SICA. The code indicates (1) logistics materiel management, (2) level of responsibility, and (3) basis of categorization.

   a. Level of Authority (LOA) Rule 22- A military service activity designated as the lead service (PICA) and assigned, as a minimum, single submitter cataloging responsibility, procurement authority, disposal authority, and depot maintenance responsibility for a multiused or single used nonconsumable item that is, major end item, depot reparable component, nonstock funded consumable special management item. Individual items, which are managed by the military services some combination of the above with a stock funded consumable are are also considered as nonconsumable items. The degree of support received by a SICA from the lead service (PICA) is is identified by the NIMSC reflected in the Segment B of the DLSCTIR.

   b. Level of Authority (LOA) Rule 8D- A military service activity designated as the SICA for a nonconsumable item (that is, major end item, depot reparable component, nonstock funded consumable/ special management item; an individual item, which is managed by the military services in some combination of the above with a stock funded consumable, is also considered as a nonconsumable item) where lead service responsibility (single submitter cataloger, procurement authority, disposal authority and maintenance responsibility) has been assigned to another service. The degree of support received from the lead service (PICA) is identified by the NIMSC reflected in segment B of the DLSC TIR.

Major Organizational Entity (MOE) Rule- A composition of various alpha/numeric codes which, in addition to identifying the MOE, identifies the subcomponent of the MOE responsible for designated materiel management functions and reflects the relationship between the subcomponents of the MOE as it pertains to logistics support obtained or provided.

Maintenance Interservice Support Management Office (MISMO)- Individual offices established at AMC, NAVSUP, AFLC, and USMC headquarters as service representatives and focal points to provide and ensure continuity and standardization of policies and procedures within and among the services for depot maintenance interservicing.

Management Level Code (MLC)- A code assigned to an item to identify the management technique being applied by the using service. Code D indicates the item is managed by the service as an item of equipment; code E as a depot reparable component; code R as a consumable; and code U special technique is applied.

Military Interdepartmental Purchase Request (MIPR)- DD Form 448 is used by the requiring Military Department to request the procurement of supplies or nonpersonal services by the procuring department or agency, and permits the procuring department or agency to authorize manufacture of the necessary supplies.

Nonconsumable Items- NSN items of supply which are major end items (principal and secondary), depot reparable components, special management, or inconsistent items.

Nonconsumable Item Management- Those materiel management functions which are centrally performed in order that an item can be introduced and managed in the DOD logistics system. Single submitter cataloger, procurement, disposal authority, and depot maintenance have been designated for single-point assignment. Other functions/processes, such as item selection, configuration control, engineering control and intermediate maintenance posturing are recognized as service mission/program related, which must be addressed individually by item by service.

Nonconsumable Item Materiel Support Codes (NIMSC)- Codes assigned to nonconsumable items which indicate the degree of materiel support obtained by the SICA from the PICA or to identify the service and/or sources of repair.

Nonconsumable Item Subgroup (NIS)- A working group comprised of military service representatives chartered by the JPCG/DIMM to develop materiel management procedures and systems for implementation of the DOD direction to eliminate duplicate wholesale inventory management of nonconsumable items.

Organic Maintenance- Maintenance performed by a military department under military control using Government-owned or controlled facilities, tools, test equipment, spares, repair parts, and military and civil service personnel.

Primary Inventory Control Activity (PICA)- The military service designated under this program as the single activity within the DOD responsible for providing materiel support under this program. Responsibilities will be discharged through normal service channels.

Secondary Inventory Control Activity (SICA)- The military services receiving materiel support under this program from the PICA for selected logistics functions. Responsibilities will be discharged through normal service channels.

Single Submitter Cataloger- For this procedure, will be defined as the activity designated as the PICA. The actual single submitter will be the activity so designated within the MOE rule. Excluded from single submitter transaction is CMD in which cataloging transactions, initiated by the PICA or SICAs, are appropriate for direct submittal to DLSC.

Special Management Items- Centrally managed items designated for special management by virtue of not fitting the existing standard systems managing major end items, depot reparable components, and consumables.

Wholesale Level of Inventory- Inventories, regardless of funding source, over which an inventory manager at the national level has asset knowledge and exercises unrestricted asset control to meet worldwide inventory management responsibilities.

Consumable Level of Inventory- An inventory, regardless of funding source, usually of limited range and depth, held only by the final element in a supply distribution system for the sole purpose of internal consumption.

Intermediate Level of Inventory- An inventory, regardless of funding source, that is required between the consumer and wholesale levels of inventory for support of a defined geographic area or for tailored support of specific consumer organizations or activities.

Retail Inventory- Supplies/materiel held below the wholesale level (the intermediate and consumer levels of inventory).

APPENDIX I

ABBREVIATIONS

AAC	Acquisition Advice Code
ADP	Automated Data Processing
AFAO	Approved Force Acquisition Objective
AMARC	Aerospace Maintenance and Regeneration Center
ASD	Assistant Secretary of Defense
ATE	Automatic Test Equipment
AUTOVON	Automatic Voice Network
CAGE	Commercial and Government Entity
CCB	Configuration Control Board
CETS	Contractor Engineering and Technical Services
CIMM	Commodity Integrated Materiel Manager
CMD	Catalog Management Data
DAAS	Defense Automated Addressing System
DAR	Defense Acquisition Regulation
DCAS	Defense Contract Administration Service
DEPSECDEF	Deputy Secretary of Defense
DIDS	Defense Integrated Data System
DIMM	Defense Integrated Material Management
DIR	Disassembly Inspection Report
DLSC	Defense Logistics Services Center
DM	Depot Maintenance
DMI	Depot Maintenance Interservice
DMISA	Depot Maintenance Interservice Support Agreement
DNA	Defense Nuclear Agency
DOD	Department of Defense
DODAAD	Department of Defense Activity Address Directory
DRO	Disposal Release Order
DSOR	Depot Source of Repair
ECP	Engineering Change Proposal
ETD	Effective Transfer Date
FAD	Force Activity/Designators
FAR	Federal Acquisition Regulation
FOSSL	Follow-on Provisioning/Outfitting
FSC	Federal Supply Class
FSG	Federal Supply Group
GFE	Government Furnished Equipment
I&S	Interchangeability and Substitutability
ICP	Inventory Control Point
IMM	Integrated Materiel Manager
IPD	Issue Priority Designator
ISIS	Interchangeable Substitutable Item Subgroup
ISSL	Initial Provisioning/Outfitting
JCAP-CG	Joint Conventional Ammunition Production-Coordinating Group
JLC	Joint Logistics Commanders

JPCG/DIMM	Joint Policy Coordinating Group for Defense Integrated Materiel Management
JSCCB	Joint Services Configuration Control Board
LOA	Level of Authority
LR	Logistics Reassignment
MILSBILS	Military Standard Billing System
MIL-STD	Military Standard
MILSTEP	Military Supply and Transportation Evaluation Procedures
MILSTRAP	Military Standard Transaction Reporting and Accounting Procedures
MILSTRIP	Military Standard Requisitioning and Issue Procedures
MIPR	Military Interdepartmental Purchase Request
MISMO	Maintenance Interservice Support Management Office
MLC	Management Level Code
MOE	Major Organizational Entity
MOV	Materiel Obligation Validation
MRO	Materiel Release Order
MSD	Materiel Support Date
NIMSC	Nonconsumable Item Materiel Support Code
NIMSR	Nonconsumable Item Materiel Support Request
NIPC	Nonconsumable Item Program Committee
NIS	Nonconsumable Item Subgroup
NSA	National Security Agency
NSN	National Stock Number
OASD	Office of the Assistant Secretary of Defense
OPR	Office of Primary Responsibility
OSD	Office of the Secretary of Defense
OWRMR	Other War Reserve Material Requirement
PHST	Packaging/Handling/Storage/Transportability
PICA	Primary Inventory Control Activity
PMC	Procurement Method Code
PR	Purchase Request
PN	Part Number
PWRR/PWRS	Prepositioned War Reserve Requirement/Preposition War Reserve Stock
QA	Quality Assurance
QDR	Quality Deficiency Report
RDEC	Requirements Data Exchange Card
SICA	Secondary Inventory Control Activity
SISMS	Standard Integrated Support Management System
SMR	Source Maintenance Recoverability
SOS	Source of Supply
TDR	Teardown Deficiency Report
TIR	Total Item Record
UMMIPS	Uniform Materiel Movement and Issue Priority System
WISSA	Wholesale Interservice Supply Support Agreement
WMR	War Materiel Requirements.

APPENDIX J

LIST OF REFERENCED DOD AND OTHER JOINT SERVICE REGULATIONS

DODD 4000.19 Interservice, Interdepartmental and Interagency Support

DOD 4000.19R Defense Regional Interservice Support (DRIS).

DOD 4000.25-1M Military Standard Requisitioning and Issue Procedures (MILSTRIP)

DOD 4000.25-2M Military Standard Transaction Reporting and Accounting Procedures (MILSTRAP)

DOD 4000.25-3M Military Supply and Transportation Evaluation Procedures (MILSTEP)

DOD 4000.25-7M Military Standard Billing System (MILSBILLS)

DOD 4100.39-M The Defense Integrated Data System (DIDS)

DOD 4120.3-M Defense Standardization and Specification Program

DOD 4130.2-M The Federal Cataloging System

DOD 4140.26-M Defense Integrated Materiel Management Manual for Consumable Items

DOD 4140.32-M Defense Inactive Item Program

DOD I4140.35 Physical Inventory Control for Department of Defense Supply System Materiel

DODI 4140.42 Determination of Initial Requirements for Secondary Item Spare and Repair Parts

DOD 4160.21-M DOD Personal Property Utilization and Disposal Program

DODI 4400.1 Priorities and Allocations

DODD 4410.6 Uniform Materiel Movement and Issue Priority System (UMMIPS)

DODD 5000.29 Management of Computer Resources in Major Defense Systems

DODD 5000.39 Acquisition and Management of Integrated Logistic Support for System and Equipment

DODI 5010.12 DOD Technical Data Management Program

DODD 5010.19 DOD Configuration Management Program

DODD 7290.1 Method of Financing, Funding, Accounting and Fiscal Reporting for the Military Assistance Grant Aid Program

DODD 7290.3-M Foreign Military Sales Financial Management Manual

DODI7420.12 Billing, Collecting and Accounting for Sales of Material from Supply System Stock

AR 700-82,   Joint Regulation Governing the Use and Application of Uniform Source
OPNAVINST 4410.2,   Maintenance and Recoverability Codes
AFR 66-45,
MCO 4400.120,
DSAR 4100.6

AFLC/AFSCR 800-24,   Standard Integrated Support Management System (SISMS)
DARCOM-R 700-97,
NAVMATINST 4000.38,
MCO P4410.1B

DLAR 4155.24, Reporting of Product Quality Deficiencies Across Component Lines
AR 702-7,
NAVMATINST 4855.8B,
AFR 74-6,
MCO 4855.5D

OPNAVINST 4790.14,   Logistics Depot Maintenance Interservice
AMC-R 750-10,
AFLCR/AFSCR 800-30,
MCO P4790.10A

www.ingramcontent.com/pod-product-compliance
Lightning Source LLC
Chambersburg PA
CBHW080538290526
45790CB00006B/2463